65

WOMEN
OF THE
BIBLE

WOMEN

OF THE

BIBLE

By

H. V. MORTON

DODD, MEAD & COMPANY
NEW YORK   1941

PRINTED IN THE UNITED STATES OF AMERICA
BY THE VAIL-BALLOU PRESS, INC., BINGHAMTON, N. Y.

Contents

[v]

CONTENTS

WOMEN
OF THE
BIBLE

Introduction

ON A brilliant day in early spring I came within sight of the palms of Beersheba. This village lies on the edge of the southern desert of Palestine, where low hills roll westward to the sand-dunes and the sea, and melt on the south into the silent yellowness of the Sinai Desert and the northern frontier of Egypt.

[1]

There are a few palm-trees in Beersheba, a bust of Lord Allenby, some forlorn huts, where the Bedouin buy groceries on credit until the barley harvest is over, and, most important of all, a law court.

The Arab, like the Irishman, loves nothing better than a lawsuit. A hearty and expensive quarrel about nothing occupies the place in desert life which the cinema and football occupy in our own civilization. Without them, life for many would be an exceedingly dull affair.

The law court, standing by itself on the sand, has the strange appearance of a provincial railway station that might have been unaccountably blown over from France. Its windows are closely guarded by green venetian shutters to exclude the burning sun, its steps are generally congested by plaintiffs and defendants, its walls are surrounded by camels, asses, and horses, and once a fortnight its halls echo to complaints which are not strange to our ears because they are to be found in *Genesis*.

In the clear air of the desert, and in that flat country, you can see a man on a camel cross the sky-line and, unless he dodges about among the hills, you can follow his slow approach every yard of the way. You may be sure, as you watch him, that he is bringing to Beersheba some dispute about camels, asses, the right to use a certain well, or perhaps some particularly dirty trick which a relative has played on him.

Abraham, Isaac, Jacob, and Esau follow each other into

the dock or the witness-box, while Moses, in a camel-hair robe, with a scimitar slung across his body on a belt of goatskin, runs a lean brown hand down his beard and gives judgment.

I heard a Bedouin utter in defence the very words which Laban uttered on the question of giving in marriage a younger daughter before an elder one:

"It is not customary for it to be so done," he said.

That is regarded as a perfectly adequate explanation in Beersheba. More men have been acquitted on the count of custom than any other. Even murder assumes a righteous aspect when it is proved that it has always been customary for members of certain tribes to slay each other on sight.

"It is customary for it to be so," they say quietly; and the judge reluctantly imposes a fine of riding-camels.

From an atmosphere so strange to a modern man, yet familiar to any student of the Old Testament, I took the path over the sand to one of the wells which Abraham dug centuries before the modern world began. These are still in use.

A girl drew near, carrying a water-pot on her shoulder. She was in that brief loveliness of youth which vanishes from an Arab maid almost as one watches. At twenty she is often middle aged; at thirty-five a wrinkled grandmother. But in her teens she sometimes justifies the rhapsodies of the Song of Songs and, standing for a moment against the ageless background of the desert, typifies in a remarkable manner all the women of the Bible.

No traveller has visited Palestine without observing this. The moment when the fellāhīn and Bedouin girls draw water from the well is a moment when, so it seems, the ghosts of Ruth and Rachel, Rebekah and Miriam, have stolen from the past into the present. And, as I looked at her, noting the fine poise of her head, so soon to be lowered beneath the yoke of motherhood, noting the pure-bred Bedouin hands, and the narrow brown feet— so like the fine narrow feet of Egyptian statues—I felt that she might have been Ruth, Rachel, or Rebekah.

I thought, as she took the cool water out of the well, of all the famous women whose lives, good and bad, are imperishably enshrined in the books of the Old and New Testaments. They form a feminine picture gallery unmatched in the whole of literature. Their histories, the diversity of their fate, and the influence which the story of their lives has exerted on the world, make them unique. Why, one may wonder, do these women, so far from us in time and so briefly described, live so vividly in the imagination? It is not merely because they happen to occur in Scripture: it is because they are so palpably alive. And I think there is perhaps another reason.

The more we know of our fellow men, and the more closely we study the lives of those who have gone before us, the more clearly do we realize that the strings of the heart are numbered, and that the harmony or the discord which life draws from us is the same old tune that has been running through the world since Mankind was born to sorrow and to joy. The change, the inventions, the fashions which are the keynote of our time, are perhaps apt to make us forget that men and women have not changed much since the age of *Genesis*.

Watching the Arab girl who seemed to symbolize all the women of the Bible, I thought that I would like to try and sketch a gallery of portraits that includes such magnificent contrasts as Ruth and Jezebel, Abigail and Delilah, Salome and Mary Magdalene.

I have stressed their common humanity and their modernness perhaps more than might have been considered proper in the last century, but that, in my opinion, is their distinctive quality. Most of us have had the opportunity of studying Martha and Mary in our own families, or among the ranks of our friends and acquaintances, some of us, no doubt, have known the devoted, firm-minded Sarah, and many are well acquainted with that monument of fierce and doting motherhood, Rebekah, or the "well favoured" Rachel, whose easy charm vanishes into an envious and petulant middle-age. Potiphar's wife moves through the newspapers in a variety of guises, and Delilah is a character known to the police and the legal profession: the female Judas who is always willing to entrap a Samson for silver.

It is indeed the whole of womanhood which is presented to us in the women of the Bible, unchanging, unvarying from age to age: a feminine portrait gallery drawn with a marvellous stark economy and unsurpassed in its variety in the whole of literature.

Eve

EVE HAS always been a convenient peg on which men have hung unflattering theories about women.

The responsibility for bringing into the world both sin and work has been cast upon her shoulders, and succeeding generations have made this charge more or less in the words of the first Adam, which are the words of a rather sneaky little boy caught out by the headmaster: "*She* gave me of the tree and I did eat."

Was it not St. Augustine who developed the theory, later employed so triumphantly by Milton, that Adam, having no desire to taste the fruit of the Tree, did so purely out of loyalty to Eve? I have a shrewd idea that it would be difficult to persuade any woman to believe this!

Artists have been more generous to Eve than writers. They have always interpreted her in the terms of their most attractive models. Nothing, I feel sure, would persuade an artist that Eve was short, fat, or myopic, that she was covered with hair, or was bow-legged, that she squinted or was afflicted with one of the eye diseases so frequent among her Eastern sisters.

Our conception of Eve is therefore woman idealized; and in this tribute the artists of the world have atoned for all the bitter things which the writers of the world have said about the first woman.

When we read with understanding the first chapters of *Genesis,* although there is no description of Eve's physical appearance, not one word to suggest whether she was fair or dark, tall or short, we do learn by inference that she was good to look at; or rather that Adam considered her so.

Adam's first reaction, when he saw her standing there in the Garden of Eden, was to give voice to the first poem, a fact which is not indicated by our translators of the Bible.

"This is now bone of my bones," he said, according to the Authorized Version, "and flesh of my flesh; she shall be called Woman because she was taken out of man." That is a bald translation of what he said.

A more exact rendering of the Hebrew original is that of Dr. James Moffatt, who sets out Adam's greeting to his wife more lyrically as:

> This, this, at last is bone of my bones,
> and flesh of my own flesh:
> This shall be called Wo-man,
> for from man was she taken!

Therefore we can conclude from Adam's sudden surprising plunge into blank verse that the sight of Eve was entirely agreeable to him.

The other day I turned from *Genesis* to Sir James Jeans's *The Mysterious Universe,* and towards the end of his brilliant exposition of modern physics, of matter and radiation, of relativity and ether, I came across the following remarks, which bring us back to the first words of the Bible, "In the beginning God created the heaven and earth."

If the universe is a universe of thought [writes Sir James Jeans], then its creation must have been an act of thought.

Indeed, the finiteness of time and space almost compel us, of themselves, to picture the creation as an act of thought; the determination of the constants such as the radius of the universe and the number of electrons it contained imply thought, whose richness is measured by the immensity of these qualities.

Time and space, which form the setting for the thought, must have come into being as part of this act. Primitive cosmologies pictured a creator working in space and time, forging sun, moon and stars out of already existent raw material. Modern scientific theory compels us to think of the creator as working outside time and space, which are part of his creation, just as the artist is outside his canvas.

Only those who still think in terms of the old-fashioned rationalism of the last century can dismiss the extraordinary story of Adam and Eve as a childish tale. The modern scientist and the modern scholar regard it as an inspired pictorial, or symbolic, description of the mystery of life, to which modern research can add a thousand theories but no conclusions.

It is interesting that Josephus and Philo, both Jews, one an historian and the other a philosopher, and both writing in the first century after Christ, regarded the Biblical account of the Creation more as Sir James Jeans does than, for instance, as Gladstone did.

They both read the first chapters of *Genesis* as St. Paul read certain incidents in the Old Testament, as fundamental spiritual truths wrapped up in easily comprehended myths.

It is a story free from the monstrous fantasy of most primitive conceptions of the Creation, and it contains truths that can be understood by the simplest, and depths that may be studied by the wisest, of mankind.

The story of the Creation is one of the most inspired allegories in the Bible. God formed man from the dust of the ground, and then He breathed into his nostrils the breath of life.

Man's dual nature was never described with a more powerful brevity. While we are of the earth, earthy, the breath of life is in us, bringing with it those spiritual and intellectual capacities that lift us from the brute creation.

Man is an exception whatever else he is [wrote G. K. Chesterton]. If he is not the image of God, then he is a disease of the dust. If it is not true that a Divine being fell, then we can only say that one of the animals went entirely off its head.

In the character of Eve various stern critics of woman have seen a creature inquisitive, weak, deceitful, and ambitious.

I do not think that, so far as moral qualities go, there was a pin to choose between Adam and Eve. They were both ordinary people. Neither do I think that women are weaker, more deceitful, more inquisitive, or more ambitious than men. The quality which Eve possessed,

[11]

which no learned commentators ever mention, and one which I think is possessed in a marked degree by all her descendants, is that of daring.

It must have taken great daring to sin for the first time. Perhaps the reason why the serpent did not go straight to Adam with his temptation, but decided with fiendish ingenuity to get at him through his wife, was because he knew perfectly well that Adam would never have had the courage to sin.

The psychology of the Temptation is well worth a closer examination than most of us have ever given to it. I do not know another brief story that seems to expand so surprisingly the more one studies it.

The serpent's approach to Eve is a masterpiece of subtle suggestion. He does not tell her to sin, but he insinuates in the cleverest way that there is really nothing at all to worry about in sin. The technique employed so successfully in Eden is one that has been busily at work ever since, and will continue to work as long as the world lasts. It is the germ of all temptation.

Hath God said: Ye shall not eat of every tree of the garden?

He opens the conversation in a casual way by asking for information which he knew perfectly well all the time. Eve answers him with shattering innocence. One can almost see the serpent grinning with amusement as he listens. The tone of his subsequent remarks then casts an indirect reflection on the generosity of God. It is hardly possible, he says in effect, that a beneficent Creator should have withheld this great experience from Adam and Eve. Can God be as good and wise as Eve supposes, if He has forbidden the eating of the Tree of Knowledge?

Many daughters of Eve have discovered that the serpent is never more dangerous than when he professes to be the earnest well-wisher interested in nothing but her advancement and welfare.

So Eve fell.

The reasons given for Eve's surrender to the serpent are illuminating. She saw that "the tree was good for food." Her bodily appetite was tempted. It "was a delight to the eyes." Her sensuous nature was tempted. She saw, thirdly, "that the tree was to be desired to make one wise." This, perhaps, was the most powerful temptation of all; the spiritual temptation to transcend the normal experience of men and to taste of the wisdom that belongs only to God.

Surely posterity has been hard on Eve. Although it is not possible to excuse her fall from grace, is it not unfair to blame her, as Milton does, for a sin which was shared in an equal degree by Adam? If Adam did not pluck the fruit, he was at least standing under the tree ready to take a bite of it:

She took of the fruit thereof and did eat and gave also to her husband with her; and he did eat.

Adam's attitude at this critical moment suggests, as many a cynic has suspected, that man is really the weaker sex. Adam did not stop Eve. There is no suggestion that he even attempted to argue with her. He just stood there and watched the headstrong woman send the whole world to work, and when he saw that she was safe he took the forbidden fruit also.

The lesson of Eve is that, for good or evil, she will lead Adam, even, or perhaps especially, when the devil prompts her.

Josephus, explaining the Jewish faith to the Roman world eighteen centuries ago, concludes the story in words that cannot be improved:

God allotted Adam punishment because he weakly submitted to the counsel of his wife. He also made Eve liable to the inconveniency of breeding. He also deprived the serpent of speech, out of indignation at his malicious disposition towards Adam. Besides this He inserted poison under his tongue and made him an enemy to men: and when He had deprived him of the use of his feet He made him go rolling all along, and dragging himself upon the ground. And when God had appointed these penalties for them, He removed Adam and Eve out of the garden into another place.

And that place is the world in which we live. The magnificent allegory works itself out on a cruel stage. Eve becomes the mother of the first murderer. And she worships him. She calls him Cain, which means "to get" or "to possess," a name that pictures her hugging the small child to her heart in the fierce joy of maternity. And her second son is Abel, which means "a breath," "a vapour," something that is doomed to fade; for Abel, unlike his brother, was sickly and weak.

There is an unwritten chapter in the life of Eve. She is the mother who sees her favourite first-born branded with shame, while the pitiful Abel becomes a martyr. The idyllic garden vanishes. The streets of London or Paris might surround her, for, in the knowledge of good and evil, she is all the women who have ever lived.

Sarah

I THINK most of the authorities agree that Abraham was born at Ur, which is now a dusty heap of ruins in Iraq called El Tell al Muqayyar, "the Mound of Pitch." The name refers to the remains of the great Ziggurat still to be seen there. The ruins stand on the flat and featureless plain about a hundred and twenty miles from the point where the Euphrates flows into the Persian Gulf.

I went there in days which now appear so distant, although only three years ago, and, after a night's train journey from Baghdad, stepped out upon a brown waste like the bed of a dried-up sea. Some two miles or so from the lonely little railway station that bore the word "Ur" so improbably upon its platform, I saw an object, the only elevation on the landscape, which, at first sight, resembled a vast collapsed chocolate blancmange. This was the Ziggurat of Nannar, the Moon Goddess, whose cult was the religion of Abraham's birthplace.

From the summit of that mighty ramp of brick, I gazed upon a scene of utter desolation. Except to the east, where the tasselled heads of palm trees outlined the curve of the distant Euphrates, the land from sky to sky was brown, flat and barren. For perhaps a distance of half a mile round the Ziggurat the archaeologists have removed the sand from the City, exposing the roofless dwellings of Ur, which, as I looked down upon them, resembled the stained and broken honeycomb which old-fashioned bee-keepers take in the autumn from straw hives. The little cell-like houses, most of them complete save for their roofs, lie together in a tangle of narrow streets; an astonishing relic of an inconceivably remote world.

It required some vision to imagine what this place was like when Abraham and Sarah lived there. If the date of Abraham's era was, as some authorities believe it to have

[18]

been, 2200 B.C., the City of Ur was already hoary with antiquity, and was indeed just about to submit itself to the upstart power of Babylon. The priests and priestesses of that time, who mounted the ramp of the Ziggurat, looked out upon no desert stretching from sky to sky, as we do to-day, but upon a fair and irrigated land planted with grain and with shady gardens. Neither was Ur an inland town. The great plain that stretches for a hundred and twenty miles to the Persian Gulf has been formed by river silt carried down by the flood waters of the Tigris and the Euphrates, each flood adding a little more to the desert and pushing the sea a little further back. But in Abraham's day sea-going ships sailed into the docks of Ur, the hot streets were invigorated by the sea wind, and the ancient city, as full of waterways as Venice, echoed to the splash of oar, and to the sweetest music in the East: the murmur of moving water.

Above the docks and the streets, above the gardens and the canals, rose the artificial mountain of brick, planted with rare trees, its massive stages zoned in primitive colours: the lower stage black, the upper stage red, and the shrine on the summit shining with glazed blue tiles and a roof of gilded metal.

In Babylonia, as in Egypt, centuries of stagnation have transformed once fertile places into deserts, and the prevailing colour of those lands is the brown of sand, so that it is easy to forget that in ancient times the temples glowed and shone with colour: in Egypt the enormous walls, the pylons, the obelisks, even the statues of gods and kings, were painted with red, blue, green, yellow and gold, and in Babylonia, too, colour, that must have been almost unbearably brilliant in the harsh sunlight of that land, was seen wherever the Ziggurats lifted their massive outlines above the palm groves.

The people of Ur have left strange reflections of themselves in the form of stone statuettes, which the archaeologists have found among the ruins and have placed in the museum at Baghdad: weird squat little men wearing sheepskin kilts, hands meekly folded on their breasts, wide eyes staring from rims of lapis-lazuli; curious friezes in which men dance with animals for the edification of the Moon Goddess, and, in contrast to the primitive statuary, superb metal work of a quality hardly surpassed by the treasure of Tut-ankh-Amûn or the gold hoard of Mycenæ.

It was in this complex, mercantile, theocratic city-state of Ur that Father Abraham began his life; a background vastly different from that of the desert on which his later life was spent. He was a member of an ancient and civilized community, and, as Sir Leonard Woolley has written, "it would be difficult to avoid the belief that his later life must have been influenced by a youth spent in such surroundings."

He lived in Ur with his father Terah and his two

brothers Nahor and Haran. Haran became the father of Lot and died at Ur. Abraham and Nahor married there: Abraham married Sarah, and Nahor married Milcah, his niece, the daughter of Haran. Why the family of Terah should have uprooted themselves from Ur and have wandered so far afield is not known. We are suddenly told that Terah, taking with him Abraham, Lot and Sarah, left Ur and journeyed to Haran far to the north. And it was in Haran that Terah died. Abraham then became head of the family, and at Haran received his first call from God.

Abraham is the first man in the Bible who is conscious of a Divine mission. Throughout his history we are always coming across the words: "the Lord said unto Abraham." When the modern Arab feels an imperative urge to do something he says: "God has spoken to me to-day." And Abraham, it would seem, was conscious of this commanding Voice directing the whole course of his life.

It would appear at first sight that Sarah is lost in the mighty shadow of her husband. But that is not so to any one who has dwelt on the words of the Bible, which have an astonishing capacity for expanding and extending themselves. Brief though the account of Sarah is, it is a full-length portrait of a real woman.

She was unusually beautiful. She was obedient. She was, in fact, the first obedient woman in Scripture. Eve paid the penalty of disobedience, and so did Lot's wife. But Sarah was of a different quality. Although on two occasions she lost her temper she never disobeyed her husband.

She was also a model wife, because, throughout a life of almost continuous travel, she never argued or asked silly questions, which is the first rule of satisfactory wayfaring. When she was told to leave her own country and journey into a strange land to help her husband to fulfil his divinely inspired destiny, she meekly followed, aware, as the whole attitude of her life proved, that Abraham was always right.

One of the greatest blessings of Abraham's life was the fact that Sarah was such an unquestioning traveller. During the course of his wandering he was to learn that it is impossible to mix travel with argument.

That was when Lot became disagreeable. And Abraham did the only sensible thing: "Separate thyself, I pray thee, from me," he said, "if thou wilt take the left hand, then I will go to the right; or if thou depart to the right hand, then I will go to the left."

Never once, however, in the course of years of travel did Sarah prove unequal to the strain. Her character is that of a practical woman. Abraham was often obscured in the clouds, but Sarah was always firmly anchored to the earth.

Like most great men, Abraham possessed several irritating habits, and one of the most annoying to Sarah must have been his continual fear that kings were going to fall in love with her. Men married to great beauties frequently exhibit this fear.

With Abraham it took the peculiar form, for which no commentator has been able to discover an excuse, of pretending that he was not married to Sarah. His idea was that, if Oriental despots knew that they were man and wife, he would be swiftly removed and Sarah would be seized by amorous monarchs.

Unfortunately Abraham misjudged the two kings who looked lovingly on Sarah. They were both perfect gentlemen. The fact that she was introduced to them as Abraham's sister had exactly the opposite effect of that intended. Sarah was immediately included in the harem, first of Pharaoh, and later of Abimelech. Learning the true relationship, however, both monarchs politely returned Sarah to her husband with a suitable rebuke.

The drama of Sarah deepens when, old and childless, she plays her part in the first recorded human triangle. It is a strange story to our Western ideas of morality.

Knowing that God had promised Abraham a numerous progeny, and unable to see herself as the mother, Sarah pressed on her husband a young Egyptian slave-girl named Hagar. This girl was Sarah's property, and, according to the custom of the time, her children would be Sarah's children.

Then something occurred so true to human nature that it is difficult to understand how any one could ever imagine that this story was fiction. In the first pages of *Genesis* we realize one of the most remarkable things about the Bible: that although we move in it through ages fantastically remote, we are moving all the time in the very heart of human nature.

As soon as Hagar knew that she, and not Sarah, was chosen to found the race of Abraham, she began to give herself airs. The humble maidservant began to look down upon her mistress. She flaunted her triumph before Sarah. But Hagar had underestimated Sarah, and overestimated the patience of Abraham. The result was that Abraham turned Hagar over to Sarah for discipline. Sarah "dealt hardly with her," and Hagar fled into the wilderness.

Men and women must, perhaps, always feel differently about Hagar and Sarah. To men, it must seem painfully illogical that Sarah, after herself suggesting the scheme, should suddenly turn round and drive Hagar out, possibly to death. It seems a typically feminine perversity; the sort of thing that has made many a man realize with despair that women often do not look directly at a thing, but all the way round it!

Women, on the other hand, and especially childless wives, must sympathize with the righteous rage of Sarah, who, already humiliated in the very core of her heart, was forced to suffer the sneering triumph of a younger woman.

Yet Hagar, driven out by Sarah and abandoned by Abraham, is one of the most touching pictures in Scripture. As if to suggest that in the most tragic tangle of human relationships there is sometimes a little right on all sides, the Angel of the Lord, finding Hagar "by the fountain in the way to Shur," bade her arise and return again to submit herself to the hands of her mistress.

So Hagar returned and became the mother of Ishmael, from whom the Arabs claim descent. And it would be difficult to better the description of them given by the Angel of the Lord as he described Ishmael:

He will be a wild man; his hand will be against every man, and every man's hand against him; and he shall dwell in the presence of all his brethren.

Every one who has travelled in Arab countries will recognize the fidelity of the description of Abraham's reception of the three divine strangers. They came to tell him that Sarah, although past the age of motherhood, should give birth to Isaac.

He was sitting at the door of his tent in the heat of the day. When he saw the strangers he rose, and like any sheikh in the desert to-day, ran to meet them from the tent door, and bowed himself toward the ground.

And Abraham hastened into the tent unto Sarah, and said, Make ready quickly three measures of fine meal, knead it, and make cakes upon the hearth. And Abraham ran unto the herd, and fetcht a calf tender and good, and gave it unto a young man; and he hasted to dress it. And he took butter, and milk, and the calf which he had dressed, and set it before them. . . .

The picture is absolutely true to life, except that to-day the sheikh rushes to make coffee and kills a sheep instead of a calf. The whole animal is stewed in a pot within sight of the tent, while your host talks to you even as Abraham talked to the three strangers; and, when ready, it is served with melted butter as Abraham served the calf.

During this meal, Sarah, sitting on the other side of the goat-hair partition, overheard her approaching destiny, and laughed aloud at the thought that she, so old and so resigned to childlessness, should become the mother of Isaac.

It is on a note of triumph that Sarah's long life ends. She becomes the proud mother of Isaac. And once again her rage blazes out against Hagar. Magnificently true to life, she becomes the mother fighting for the rights of her own child:

"Cast out this bondwoman and her son," she cries, "for

the son of this bondwoman shall not be the heir with my son, even with Isaac."

This cry completes the portrait of Sarah, a woman masterful yet obedient, intolerant of rivalry yet capable of self-sacrifice, practical to the last degree yet possessed of those qualities of the mind which, in an age when a childless woman was often put away as a worthless thing, made her the cherished and unrivalled companion of her husband.

Lot's Wife

"His wife looked back from behind him, and became a pillar of salt."

That is surely the shortest biography in literature. It is nearly all we know of Lot's Wife; yet that single sentence has placed her among the famous women of the world.

Thousands of years after the destruction of Sodom and Gomorrah, Lot's Wife was remembered by Jesus Christ. It is the only mention of her in the New Testament. When Jesus was warning His followers of the approaching destruction of Jerusalem, He instructed them to fly to the hills when the time of danger should come, telling them not to pause even to take up the goods from their houses. "Remember Lot's Wife," He said.

From that day until this the name of Lot's Wife has symbolized the destruction which overtakes those who, faced with salvation, turn to gaze back longingly on material things.

I think the few verses of *Genesis* that describe the destruction of Sodom and Gomorrah are among the most powerful and the most vivid in the whole Bible. If I had to run one of those schools which are supposed to teach people how to write, I would tell my pupils to read and learn this chapter until they knew it by heart, for never has a mighty disaster, the sound of it, the smell, the smoke, and the horror of it, been painted in fewer and more pregnant words.

George Adam Smith called it "the popular and standard judgment of sin." He was right, too, in his statement that the glare of those burning cities is flung right down the whole length of Biblical history.

The story told in *Genesis* is applied in *Deuteronomy,* is driven home by Amos, by Isaiah, by Jeremiah, by

Ezekiel. Jesus Christ employs it as the pattern of judgment. St. Paul, St. Peter, and St. Jude each mentions it,
and in the Apocalypse the name of Sodom is the name of
the great city of sin.

Before I went to Palestine I believed that this terrible
episode was a legend framed in remote times to drive
home to primitive minds the penalty of transgression.

The Old Testament, as St. Paul noted, contains several
stories which are not true in any but a spiritual sense;
that is to say, they never actually happened, but were set
down in that particular narrative form as the best and
strongest way to drive home a truth. This, I believed, was
the explanation of the nineteenth chapter of *Genesis*.

Any one who journeys down from Jerusalem to the
Dead Sea must change his mind about this. In half an
hour, going steadily downhill all the way, you leave the
highlands of Judaea and come into a terrible lost world
which will always be one of Nature's strangest freaks.
One glance tells you that this country was formed by some
mighty convulsion of the earth.

The Dead Sea, in which nothing can live, in which no
body can sink, which is like a sheet of blue metal on calm
days, which is so salt that, if you dip your hand in it and
hold it in the air, it becomes white with encrusted chemicals in a few seconds, is the strangest sheet of water in the
world.

It lies thirteen hundred feet below sea-level, and the

few huts round it, and a chemical factory at the northern end, are the lowest inhabited places on the globe.

Great banks of chemicals have accumulated in the course of centuries, forming white and grey ridges. In some places the smell of sulphur is nauseating. There are grey, slimy knolls and hummocks on which nothing will ever grow; and there are banks of hard rock in which the glittering minerals shine like points of steel.

The sea that lies between these sterile, ghostly hills is called *Bahr Lut,* or the Sea of Lot, by the Arabs, and somewhere along the stricken shores of that unearthly desolation Sodom and Gomorrah once stood.

It was believed for centuries that both cities lie beneath the Dead Sea. The Arabs say that on calm days you can see their ruined walls glimmering under the salt-laden waters. But this is not true. It is imagination. The Dominican Fathers, who are the best archaeologists in Palestine, believe that Sodom and Gomorrah stood somewhere round the north end of the Dead Sea; and that is where they intend to dig for them.

Legend, however, has placed them to the south, where a great pillar of salt used to be pointed out as the figure of Lot's Wife. Salt in enormous quantities is still mined in this part of the Dead Sea. In the salt quarries near "Lot's Wife," and from the salt pans at Athlit on the coast, a company produces some seven thousand tons of salt every year.

Lot and his wife are an extremely interesting contrast to Abraham and Sarah, to whom they were related, and with whose history their life-story should be read. Like so many characters in the Old Testament, they are immortal in their common human frailty. Although they lived thousands of years before history began, you and I know people exactly like them to-day.

Neither Lot nor his wife was a bad character; in fact, Lot was full of decent feeling. He was consumed by the desire to get on in life, to become prosperous and to enjoy all the good things. When Abraham gave him the choice of turning to the left or right, Lot turned without hesitation to the rich, fat, hot plains of the Jordan Valley.

Lot dwelled in the cities of the plain and pitched his tent toward Sodom. But the men of Sodom were wicked and sinners before the Lord exceedingly.

But it did not matter to him that the cities of the plain were sinks of iniquity. All that mattered was that life was going to be easy and profitable. And Lot had married a woman as easy-going and as materially minded as himself. We learn that his daughters were married to the men of Sodom.

Prosperous, comfortable men like Lot are of two kinds: those who go to pieces in adversity and those who seem to fling off their worldliness and come through the fire. When faced with the destruction of everything he had won, Lot showed real courage in barring his gate against the men of Sodom and in flying empty-handed from the scene of his success.

But when the frightful eruption shook the Jordan Valley, when on that distant morning the mountains fell apart to form the semi-tropical cleft that runs north into Galilee, Lot's wife, unable to bring herself to part from the ease and the comfort of the good days, and disregarding the command, "Look not behind thee," paused in her flight.

She turned to gaze back on the city, wishing perhaps that she could run back and snatch something from the burning walls of her home. And in that unfortunate moment she became the pillar that has salted many a moral.

Rebekah

A FILE OF ten camels moved north into Samaria from the yellow plain round Beersheba and, crossing the green hills of Galilee, mounted into the highlands of the Lebanon, where the snow lies even in the summer time.

The ruby points of the camp-fire shone by night along the ancient highway to Damascus. Then the caravan, crossing the great desert, came after many days to the banks of the Euphrates and, moving still to the north, went onward to the city of Haran.

Leading the caravan was Eliezer of Damascus, the steward of Abraham. He was journeying at the command of his aged master to discover among the patriarch's kinsfolk a suitable wife for Isaac.

We are inclined to forget that the Israelites in Palestine were invaders of a country already occupied by many people. Abraham's sense of his strangeness in an alien land burst forth in a human, pitiful way when Sarah, the companion of his long life, lay dead before him in Kirjath-arba.

And Abraham stood up from before his dead, and spake unto the sons of Heth, saying, I am a stranger and a sojourner with you: give me a possession of a burying-place with you, that I may bury my dead out of my sight.

And again the same consciousness that he was not at home in Canaan comes out when the time arrived for Isaac to marry.

I will make thee swear by the Lord, the God of heaven, and the God of the earth [he says to his steward], that thou shalt not take a wife unto my son of the daughters of the Canaanites, among whom I dwell, but thou shalt go into my country, and to my kindred, and take a wife unto my son, Isaac.

[36]

This is the first indication of that clash between the Israelite and the Canaanite cultures that runs through a large part of the Bible. It begins with Abraham's clannish desire for Isaac to marry a kinswoman, and it develops into the great social clash between the communistic Israelites and the capitalistic Canaanites; between the worship of Jehovah and the shameful rites of Baal.

The story of the steward who went in search of a wife for Isaac and discovered Rebekah at the well is one of the most lovely idylls in the Bible, the twenty-fourth chapter of *Genesis*.

It was evening. It was the time when the women come out from the city gates with pitchers on their shoulders to draw water from the well, and above them in the brief twilight of the east the first star burned in the sky.

The dusty caravan halted before the walls of Haran. Eliezer made the weary camels kneel and, after praying that the bride of his master's son might be revealed to him, settled down to watch "the daughters of the men of the city."

The inner voice had told him that the girl who gave him drink and offered to water his tired beasts would be the girl destined for Isaac. Rebekah came to the well, a girl "very fair to look upon," and she went down the steps of the well and filled her pitcher.

"Let me, I pray thee, drink a little water of thy pitcher," asked Eliezer.

"Drink, my lord," answered Rebekah, "and I will draw water for thy camels also, until they have done drinking."

Any one who has seen a thirsty camel slake his thirst will not underrate the courtesy of Rebekah. As she filled and refilled her pitcher, giving water to the ten camels, the steward knew that she was the chosen bride. He took the emblems of betrothal and pressed them upon the wondering maid: a gold ring of half a shekel's weight, and two bracelets of ten shekels' weight of gold. Then the scene moves into the house of her relatives.

In this episode, as in the story of the three strangers in the tent of Abraham, one appreciates the unchanging attitude of the East. The interview might be taking place in a Bedouin tent to-day.

The first thought of Rebekah's family is to give hospitality to the stranger and to find fodder and straw for his camels. If you ride up to an Arab encampment to-day, food and hospitality will be offered and no one will ask your name or your business. It is not etiquette to ask such questions for three days. Hospitality always precedes inquiry. So it was thousands of years ago when Eliezer went seeking a bride for Isaac.

But the steward was so full of his mission, and so happy to realize its success, that he refused to fall in with the usual procedure.

"I will not eat until I have told mine errand."

He tells the story of his mission and distributes the

[38]

gifts so dear to the Eastern heart. Then Rebekah, faced with instant departure from the bosom of her family, is called and asked.

"Wilt thou go with this man?"

And she said, "I will go."

From which we are at liberty to assume that Rebekah was both beautiful and decisive. So the caravan set out for the distant south; and went on for weeks and for months.

And Isaac went out to meditate in the field at eventide: and he lifted up his eyes, and saw, and, behold, the camels were coming—and Rebekah lifted up her eyes, and when she saw Isaac, she lighted off her camel. For she had said unto the servant, What man is this that walketh in the field to meet us? And the servant had said, It is my master: therefore she took a veil and covered herself.

What a superb touch that is. At the sight of her bride-groom, she veiled her face.

And Isaac brought her into his mother Sarah's tent, and took Rebekah, and she became his wife; and he loved her.

So ends the exquisite poem of the meeting of Isaac and his bride.

Rebekah was younger than her husband. May it have been the quarter of a century that separated them and grew wider as Isaac aged, that explains the estrangement expressed so dramatically by Rebekah's cruel deception? The sweetest love stories do not always last. Rebekah in middle life, the mother of twins, was a different character from the young bride who rode south so gaily to meet her lover in Canaan.

There are some women, and Rebekah is the first on record, who develop a fanatic passion for their children which far outweighs any love they ever felt for their husbands. Motherhood came to her late in life, and by that time Isaac was an old man. All the longing stored up for years was poured out by Rebekah in the violence of her maternity. How violent it was can be gathered from the fact that she championed one twin against the other.

So real are the four characters in this drama that one naturally takes sides with poor old Isaac, blind and helpless, against the scheming of Rebekah. It seems to us difficult to understand how even an infatuated mother, and there are no deeper depths in infatuation, could prefer the smooth, spoilt Jacob to the honest, hairy Esau.

From the first moment of his life, when his infantile hand tried to catch at the heel of Esau and pull him back, Jacob, in his dealings with his brother, secondly in his deception of his father, thirdly in his sharp practice with the peeled wands, exhibits the regrettable character of a business man who is ready to double-cross his adversary.

How much of this was due to Rebekah's influence, and to what extent his personality, which she loved so much, should make us revise our opinion of the sweet maid from the Euphrates, I am not prepared to say.

The fact remains that Rebekah's plot to obtain the birthright of her eldest son, Esau, for her favourite, Jacob, remains one of the classic deceptions in history.

One remark of Rebekah's seems to illuminate her with a flash of almost tragic light. When Jacob objects that he cannot steal his brother's blessing because his old blind father will feel his smooth skin, which is not rough and hairy like that of Esau, his mother cuts him short and tells him to slay two kids, whose skins she will place on his hands and his neck.

"I shall bring a curse upon me, and not blessing," says the fearful Jacob; and Rebekah replies:

"Upon me be thy curse, my son, only obey my voice."

That is almost the last picture we are given of this woman. It is the picture of a strong-minded, decisive girl, who has grown into an autocratic matriarch. Whatever love she once bore her aged husband vanished when children came. Her one passion is her favourite son. There is nothing she would not do for his sake. And in his scheming, clever life we seem to see an extension of the less worthy qualities of his mother.

Rachel

It HAS been said that love does not enter the Bible until the Song of Songs. Surely it is difficult to accept this.

The love of Sarah and Abraham was a real thing. Two people do not live without children for more than a normal lifetime unless they are bound by a love that has deepened into companionship.

[43]

It is true that no recorded word of love passed between them, but more eloquent than any word of love was the cry that was torn from the heart of the aged Abraham when he saw lying dead before him the woman who had accompanied him through so many years.

"I am a stranger and sojourner with you," he cried to the men of Heth, and the cry is terrible because it is so unlike the self-sufficiency of the patriarch. But what greater tribute than this sudden unguarded cry of loneliness could he have paid to the love he felt for Sarah?

If any one argues that this is not romantic love as we know it, let me point to Jacob and Rachel. If their story is not romantic enough to stand beside those of Tristan and Isolde, Aucassin and Nicolette, Hero and Leander, and a dozen others, then I am afraid that I do not understand romance.

Most people will agree with me that no man in his right senses would agree to become a shepherd for seven years in the hope of winning a certain woman unless he were madly and romantically in love with her.

In case there was the slightest loophole for doubt, we know that Jacob, when cheated of Rachel, went on working for another seven years for her, making a total of fourteen, during which he slaved, madly and insanely in love. That Rachel was entirely unworthy of this prolonged infatuation entitles her to a front place among the romantic illusions.

Jacob is one of the most contradictory characters in the Old Testament. There is no doubt in my mind that his character was ruined by his mother, Rebekah. As we have seen, he was her favourite son, and for his sake she hatched the wicked plot to gain Isaac's blessing.

While a young man he had bought his brother's birthright with a mess of pottage. Much criticism has been directed at Esau for his weakness in selling his birthright, but how few people have ever censured the sharp practice of Jacob in taking such a mean advantage of his brother's exhaustion.

In the consistent selfishness of Jacob we may discern indication of the commercial prosperity that was to descend upon him. Morality is a matter of fashion, and it may seem to us strange that the tricks of Jacob are not condemned. We are led to believe that he must have possessed hidden spiritual qualities known only to the Creator, for the qualities by which we know him are so businesslike that, even when wrestling, and discovering that his adversary is an angel, he sees a chance of profit and cries: "I will not let thee go, except thou bless me."

Nobody but Jacob, when in the embarrassing position of having the best of a supernatural being, would have thought of trying to drive a bargain with his opponent.

The one surprising side of Jacob's character was his tenacious love for Rachel.

The modern psycho-analyst would unhesitatingly diagnose this love affair as the Oedipus complex. Jacob was one of those men on whose character an infatuated mother had impressed her mark so firmly that his search in life was to find another woman exactly like her. In this he was lucky. Rachel and Rebekah are astonishingly alike. They both form a charming picture in youth that changes in later life, as the less admirable qualities in their natures come to the front.

Rachel was unusually lovely, but no great qualities of the mind made her beautiful. Her elder sister, Leah, was "tender-eyed"; but Rachel was "well-favoured."

As in most of those Old Testament stories, we feel that we are moving in modern times, for, as I have said before, we are dealing with the human heart, and this has not changed. A modern novelist could take this situation and transpose it into our own day, and make of it a drama that would grip the attention until the last.

Leah loved Jacob. There is no indication that Rachel loved him as much. But Jacob, infatuated by the beauty of the younger sister, bound himself to the father, Laban, for seven years, at the end of which he was to receive his daughter Rachel.

Running through this love story is a strange sub-plot. Jacob, the man of wits, met his match in Laban. Laban was a greedy, dishonest man, and it seems that, in encountering his dishonesty and suffering his deception, Jacob was paying the penalty for having stolen his brother's birthright. At the end of his seven years' labour Jacob was tricked into marriage with Leah. She is the most tragic figure in the drama. She genuinely loved her husband; but still his eyes and his mind turned always to her sister.

Rachel, even after marriage with Jacob, remains one of those women with nothing to recommend her but beauty. She is bitter, envious, quarrelsome and petulant. The full force of her hatred is directed against her sister, Leah.

The horrors of polygamy are vividly sketched in the constant jealousy and bickering that goes on in the domestic quarters, as, one by one, the children of Israel enter the world.

One begins to feel sorry for Jacob. Torn between two women, one who loved him with tearful insistence, and the other whom he loved with a dog-like devotion, his life was also complicated by subsidiary handmaidens, whose abundant fruitfulness cast new discords into the patriarchal tents.

By the fact that he compressed the arguments, the difficulties, the quarrels and the misunderstandings of at least four married lives into one lifetime, one feels that he was adequately paying for the sins of his youth.

It was not the first, as it will not be the last, time that an entirely unworthy woman has enchained the lifelong affection of a man; and there is no doubt that Jacob either never saw through Rachel or else, comprehending her, he still could not help loving her.

Probably he could see no evil in her just as he could see no evil in his mother, Rebekah. He loved Rachel with the same explicit devotion.

When he fled from Laban with his wives and his great possessions, Rachel stole her father's household gods, the mascots which presided over his life. Laban set off in hot pursuit, but Rachel deceived him with supreme cunning, sitting on the camel bags in which the stolen images were concealed.

But one must feel a tardy generosity towards Rachel for two reasons: the fact that she was the mother of Joseph, a man whose virtues and whose mind shine out over the last chapters of *Genesis,* and because of the manner of her death.

She is said to be the first woman in history to die in childbirth. Before her eyes closed for ever she heard her child called Ben-oni, "the child of my sorrow," but his father called him Benjamin, "the son of the right hand."

Many years afterwards, when Jacob's life had turned to righteousness, when he was old and ill and on the point of death, his last thoughts turned to the lovely woman whose beauty had dominated his life.

Jacob was a great man, a seer, a man whose wild youth had been wiped out by the virtue of his later life. But all these things he forgot. His thoughts turned to the only woman he had loved, and from his heart came the cry:

"And as for me, when I came from Padan, Rachel died by me in the land of Canaan in the way, when yet there was but a little way to come unto Ephrath: and I buried her there in the way of Ephrath; the same is Bethlehem."

It is one of the most poignant remarks in Scripture. His sons are now fathers. Even Benjamin, the youngest, is grown up. But the thoughts of Jacob go down the years and into the tomb where Rachel lies. . . .

This building is a small, domed shrine on the right of the road as you go from Jerusalem to Bethlehem. It is one of those shrines that are sacred to Christian, to Jew, and to Moslem. Inside are flags and banners set round a huge stone tomb which tradition says marks the place where Rachel was laid to rest.

Potiphar's Wife

THERE WAS some scholarly excitement in the middle of the last century when it was believed that the original story of Joseph and Potiphar's Wife had been discovered.

This was an ancient Egyptian manuscript, written thousands of years before Christ and now in the British Museum, containing a romance called "The Brothers."

Two brothers, one married and the other a bachelor, lived happily together on a farm. The wife of the elder brother fell in love with the younger and made proposals which he rejected. Angry and insulted, the woman then staged a piece of deception and, rushing dishevelled to her husband, told him that his brother had attempted to make love to her.

The husband then pursued his brother with a reed-cutting knife, and would have caught him if the Sun God had not cast between them a canal full of crocodiles. This gave them both a pause for conversation. The younger brother managed to proclaim his innocence, whereupon the elder brother ran back to the farm, slew his wife and flung her body to the dogs.

Modern scholarship, however, recognizes no link at all between the *Papyrus d'Orbiney* and the story of Potiphar's Wife. It is realized that the erring wife is one of the commonest figures in the literature of all ages, and that she had appeared in Egypt long before Joseph set foot in that country.

For instance, the wife of the magician Ubaner, who lived in the reign of Kheops, the builder of the Great Pyramid, deceived her husband. Her lover was eaten by a magic crocodile, specially prepared for the task, and she was burned to death.

Unlike most of her predecessors, Potiphar's Wife seems to have escaped punishment.

The story of Joseph and Potiphar's Wife takes us from the simple, patriarchal world of flocks and herds into the life of cities and palaces. We pass from the deserts and the hills of Palestine to the sophisticated streets of the Egyptian capital.

Dean Stanley said that the appearance of Joseph in Egypt is the first distinct point of contact between sacred and secular history.

When you are travelling in Palestine, from Nablus, the ancient Shechem, to Nazareth, you notice on the right of the road an ancient well that has not changed its name since Old Testament days. The Arabs call it Tell Dothan. Even the spelling has not altered.

"And Joseph went after his brethren and found them at Dothan" we are told in *Genesis*.

The old well at Dothan may be the very pit into which the jealous brothers cast Joseph after stripping him of his coat of many colours. And through Dothan also passed the old caravan road used by the merchants from Petra with their loads of perfume, incense, and bitumen.

There was an enormous market in Egypt for those materials. Dead Sea bitumen was used by embalmers in the art of mumification, and the amount of incense consumed annually on the altars of the Egyptian temples must have been tremendous. It was Solomon who first saw the commercial possibilities of Arabia and, in organizing the traffic and building up his fabulous wealth, he became the first great Jewish merchant prince.

In Joseph's time, however, the big Solomonic combine had not been formed, and the Ishmaelite, or Midianite, merchants were small traders travelling with their camels from the lonely steppes of Trans-Jordan. They would be just the people willing to pick up a well-built young slave, and, passing through Dothan, disappear with him along the old trade route across the Plain of Sharon, where they would strike the ancient sea road that led south into Egypt.

Joseph's story, which concludes the *Book of Genesis,* forms part of the most noble literature that has survived from the past. It is also among the earliest examples of historical prose writing. On its human side, it is a story whose changes have been rung ever since: the story of a poor young man who goes to a strange country, where he becomes, in due time, rich and powerful, and is eventually revealed to his wondering kinsmen as the once de-spised brother.

The student of history, reading this story, notes with admiration the deft, natural manner in which the mighty background of Egypt is sketched. We leave the hills and the deserts of Canaan and see Pharaoh on his throne, sur-rounded by his ministers of state. We hear for the first time in the Bible the mention of a chariot. We encounter the Nile and the water buffaloes of the Nile, which were the fat and the lean kine of Pharaoh's dream. We learn of the great granaries which, more than once in Egyptian history, saved the land from starvation during years when the Nile failed to inundate the country.

In this story we note that the fashion of shaving the face is first mentioned in the Bible.

Then Pharaoh sent and called Joseph, and they brought him hastily out of the dungeon: and he shaved himself and changed his raiment and came in unto Pharaoh.

This is a life-like detail. In all the millions of tomb reliefs and temple pictures of Egypt there was never discovered one bearded Egyptian. The race was clean-shaven, and the fashion never changed. Only barbarians and inferior races are shown in Egyptian sculpture as bearded men.

In this vivid little sidelight we see Joseph in the white pleated garments of his adopted country, shaved and perfumed, an Egyptian in all save his blood.

Potiphar's Wife occupies an interesting place as the first sensualist in the gallery of scriptural women. The sins against morality committed by women up to this point in the Bible story were committed for dynastic reasons, or were due to the customs of the time.

And Joseph was a goodly person, and well favoured. And it came to pass after these things that his master's wife cast her eyes upon Joseph.

The immortal story of the temptation creates for us a picture of a woman, spoilt, rich, and beautiful, the product of a luxurious and licentious civilization.

In that far-gone period when Joseph lived, moral restraint was much weaker than it is to-day [wrote W. J. Dawson in *The Divine Challenge*], and the mere pagan joy of life was much stronger. Consider what it meant for such a youth to be suddenly introduced to the corrupting and luxurious life of Egypt. From the simple patriarchal life of the plains he was violently separated by a series of bitter vicissitudes.

He was a peasant of genius, suddenly made a citizen of a complex civilization; and such an instance as that of Robert Burns may serve to remind us of the grave perils of the position. If he had ever sighed for a larger life than that of the agriculturist and cattle breeder, now he had it. If he ever felt his veins athirst for the pleasures of life, now that thirst might be easily gratified. He was among a people who loved pleasure, and who knew little of sin. The standards by which they measured life were wholly different from those to which he had been accustomed.

Probably there was not one among his acquaintances who would not have laughed at his scruples, and have jeeringly told him to do in Egypt as Egypt did.

But the lesson of Joseph's renunciation is that an upright man must be true to himself, no matter what the penalty may be.

And he left his garment in her hand and fled, and got him out.

[56]

The flight underlines the strength of a character with no flaw in it.

Potiphar's Wife may have been the first woman, but she is not the last, to exhibit the classic retaliation of the woman scorned. What has been called her "love" for Joseph turned into violent hate. With masterly restraint, the writer of this chapter of *Genesis* refrains from drawing any moral from the story, but allows the action of Potiphar's Wife to speak for itself. She slanders her lover, and Joseph is cast into prison.

Potiphar's Wife is a woman known to all ages of the world's history. She appears for the first time exactly as she appeared yesterday, and she will appear to-day and to-morrow. She was vanquished by Joseph's shattering honesty in calling a spade a spade. She might have called it "romance," but he said, "How can I do this great wickedness and *sin against God.*"

If one had to preach a sermon about Potiphar's Wife, I feel that one would enlarge on the antiseptic qualities of plain speech.

Pharaoh's Daughter

THE STORY of Pharaoh's Daughter, and the finding of Moses, is one of the most perfect in the Bible. It is indeed so beautiful that one is apt to see only the story-book side of it and to forget the great historic fact that the most powerful religious force of the Old Testament owed its preservation to this incident.

[59]

It is interesting that the last chapters of *Genesis* should give us two extremely vivid portraits of Egyptian women: Potiphar's Wife and Pharaoh's Daughter. The first exhibits the undisciplined forces of womanhood in their most violent form; the second, compensating for this dark picture, reveals to us a woman tender and compassionate.

Few stories learned in childhood linger so exquisitely in the memory as the story of the princess who found among the reeds of the river bank a little ark with a young child inside it.

The interval in time which is supposed to have elapsed between *Genesis* and *Exodus* is four hundred years. Joseph, the Hebrew, who became powerful in the land of the Pharaohs and gathered his brethren round him, died at a ripe old age, was mummified and laid to rest in a painted tomb like any Egyptian noble. This is described in the last verse of *Genesis*.

With that book we leave behind the patriarchal age, and the vivid biographies of the desert potentates, and plunge into the history of a nation.

And the children of Israel were fruitful, and increased abundantly, and multiplied, and waxed exceeding mighty; and the land was filled with them. Now there arose up a new king over Egypt, which knew not Joseph.

If we are right in believing that the Pharaoh of the *Exodus* was Merenptah, then his predecessor, the oppressor of the Israelites, must have been the great Rameses II., whose victorious monuments cover the land of Egypt and whose royal name, or cartouche, is seen carved on hundreds of temples.

He noticed with alarm that the Semites from Canaan were increasing at a rate which he considered dangerous and he therefore made a law as cruel as that of Herod, a law that commanded every male child to be flung into the Nile.

Josephus gives us a number of legends connected with the birth of Moses which are not mentioned in *Exodus*. He says that, just as Herod was warned of the birth of Christ by the Wise Men, so Pharaoh was warned by Egyptian magicians that one who was to become a deliverer and lawgiver of a nation was to rise in Egypt. Therefore he determined to exterminate all male Israelites.

One mother, however, resolved to save her child from death. She hid him for three months and then, unable any longer to conceal him, made a little cradle of reeds daubed with pitch in which she placed him secretly among the rushes at the river's bank.

The translators of the Authorized Version have by the rendering of one word created a picture, very dear to the British heart, of the infant Moses cradled among bulrushes; but, alas, this picture is not accurate.

The child was placed in an ark formed of plaited papyrus reeds made watertight with a coating of bitumen. It

was believed that this plant was a protection against crocodiles.

Dr. James Moffatt in his *New Translations of the Bible*
renders this passage as:

When she could hide him no longer, she took a creel made
of papyrus reeds, daubed it over with bitumen and pitch,
and put the child in it, laying it among the reeds at the side
of the Nile.

The words for water plants have presented great difficulty to the translators of the Bible. For instance, in
Isaiah, chapter 18, verse 2, this word "gôme," which is
used to describe the cradle of Moses, is again rendered in
the Authorized Version as "bulrushes" when it should ob-
viously be "papyrus."

The "vessels of bulrushes" were the little rafts of papyrus reeds, the earliest form of craft used on the Nile,
which were greatly admired by the Greeks in later times.
Rafts similar to these are still used in the Sudan.

Therefore we must imagine the young Moses cradled
not among plants which suggest an English stream, but
among the feathery greenness that edged the ancient
Nile.

How brief but how vivid is the story of Pharaoh's
daughter!

And the daughter of Pharaoh came down to wash herself
at the river; and her maidens walked along at the river's

side; and when she saw the ark among the flags, she sent her maid to fetch it. And when she had opened it, she saw the child: and, behold, the babe wept. And she had compassion on him. . . .

She sent her attendants to find a Hebrew woman to nurse and care for the child. The mother of Moses, who was no doubt fearfully watching the fate of her precious cradle, came forward and, with beating heart, took the child to her breast.

The infant then became the special care of the king's daughter. "And she called his name Moses: and she said Because I drew him out of the water."

The name of the great leader has been thought to have been derived from two words "mo" (water), and "ushe" (saved), but modern scholars claim that the word comes from the Egyptian "mes" or "mesu," son or child.

Pharaoh's daughter is one of my favourite Bible women, firstly, I suppose, because of the beauty of this episode, and secondly, because her brief appearance underlines the importance of the apparently trivial and the apparently accidental.

There are mightier and more famous female characters in the Bible, but Pharaoh's daughter rings true as a woman, tender, kindly, and brave. In saving the small child, she proved herself ready to defy the cruel edict of her father.

"And, behold, the babe wept. And she had compassion on him."

Could the scene have been drawn more brilliantly in a page of words?

Then how true and life-like is the sudden transition from pity to the second thought: "I have found him and he belongs to me. What shall I call him?"

Her achievement in saving the life of Moses, in offering him royal protection, and in educating him in one of the great priestly colleges, is one of the most important acts in the Bible. It will occur to many that her steps were guided to the Nile. . . .

I have often had this thought when walking along the Thames Embankment. If Rameses II was the Pharaoh during the childhood of Moses, and if Moses, as it is supposed, was a young priest in the Temple of the Sun in Heliopolis, he must have walked many a time past that tall black stone which we call Cleopatra's Needle.

It has nothing to do with Cleopatra. It was carved centuries before that queen was born to commemorate the greatness of Thothmes III. Later in history Rameses the Great, who may have been the father of the princess, performed a trick for which he was notorious: he tried to obliterate the name of his predecessor, and inserted his own instead.

So Cleopatra's Needle may have stood with others at the entrance to the great Temple of the Sun when Moses, as a young priest with shaven head, went daily to learn the wisdom of the Egyptians.

Rahab

THOUSANDS OF years ago Joshua looked down on the Jordan Valley from the Mountains of Moab. He saw a flat plain lying in the heat of the sun. It looked as though the land between him and the mountains opposite had sunk deep into the earth in order to form that sun-stricken trench where even the breeze was hot, and where barley was ready for harvest in March.

Through the khaki hummocks and brushwood of this hot valley, a thin strip of green marked the course of the Jordan as it ran south from Galilee into the heavy waters of the Dead Sea.

Rising abruptly from the plain, like a yellow wall, were the mountains of Judaea, scored by dry water-channels and cut by valleys leading up to a ridge on which one day Jerusalem was to be built.

More immediately interesting to Joshua than this relief map of the Promised Land was a town standing in a dense palm forest. Mud walls twenty feet in height surrounded it and gates were set at intervals in the wall. This was Jericho. It was the first town in the path of the invading Israelites.

Joshua called two men and told them to go down into the plain and spy out the land:

"Go view the land," he said, "even Jericho."

"And they went and came into an harlot's house named Rahab, and lodged there."

Josephus and many Jewish scribes have attempted to tone down the profession of Rahab to that of "innkeeper," but the reasons are not convincing. New Testament writers have mentioned Rahab as an instance of the saving virtues of faith, and they have almost stressed her profession, notably in the *Epistle to the Hebrews* (xi. 31) and the *Epistle of James* (ii. 25).

It seems to me that the moral lessons which writers for

many thousands of years have attached to this story lose their point if Rahab of Jericho is regarded as an innkeeper.

Her house was, we learn from the second chapter of the *Book of Joshua,* "upon the town wall." This does not mean that the house was built on top of the wall. What is meant is that it was built against the town wall, so that its roof was probably level, or almost level, with the ramparts.

There are still old houses inside the city of Jerusalem like that. One that immediately comes to mind is the American Colony's Baby Home. This house is built against the town wall near the Damascus Gate. The stairway leads up to a flat roof that might almost be a continuation of the wall. No doubt this was the kind of house in which Rahab lived.

The people of Jericho spotted the suspicious strangers and noted the house in which they were staying. It is obvious that the atmosphere of Jericho in those days was as nervous as it would be to-day if forty thousand Bedouin were lying opposite in the hills of Trans-Jordan waiting for a chance to swoop down and raid the Jordan Valley.

In the darkness that night men knocked on Rahab's door.

And the King of Jericho sent unto Rahab, saying, Bring forth the men that are come to thee, which are entered into thine house; for they be come to search out all the country.

But Rahab was not willing to give the spies away. She

hid them and put the messengers on a false trail. She told them that just as dusk fell, when the city gates were shut, her two visitors had left the house and the town.

No sooner had the messengers gone than she found a more secure hiding-place for the spies. She took them to the roof of the house and hid them under stalks of flax which were drying there.

It has been assumed from the presence of flax on the roof, and also from the scarlet thread which comes later into the story, that Rahab carried on the trade of a dyer. The presence of the drying flax is eloquent also of the heat of the Jordan Valley, which was as great in Joshua's time as it is to-day. We know that the Israelite invasion occurred in Passover time, which is March or April, yet already the flax was ready in the heat of the Jericho country and already, we learn, it was harvest time.

The subsequent story is one of the most dramatic in the Old Testament. As a child one reads it as an adventure story; in later life one examines the deeper side of it. Who, I wonder, as a child, has not with breathless interest assisted in imagination at the escape of the spies from Rahab's house, watching them swing down on the rope over the town wall, touch ground and melt away into the shadows of night?

But before Rahab helped the strangers to escape she made the declaration of faith that has given this Canaanite woman a unique position among the women of the Bible.

She declared her passionate conviction in the God of Israel:

"The Lord your God, he is God in heaven above, and in earth beneath."

She talked to them by night on the roof of her house as they lay hidden in the stems of flax.

If you have ever spent a night in Jericho, it is easy to imagine this dramatic scene. The Passover moon would be growing to the full and hot winds would be rustling the palm trees. The moonlight would fall like green rain over the town of Jericho and would shine for a moment on the helmet of some watchful sentinel as he paced the wall and gazed into the hot and threatening night.

It was an extraordinary conversation in the moonlight above the walls of Jericho. It was almost like an incident from the New Testament. In that same simple, direct way, the followers of Christ professed themselves ready to sever the links with their old lives and to follow Him.

Rahab asked the spies to spare her and her relatives when Joshua conquered Jericho, and the spies swore by the God of Israel to do so. They told her to display a scarlet thread from the window, so that the attacking forces would recognize it and be able to save her house from destruction.

When all was silent, and the moon perhaps was hidden behind a bank of cloud, Joshua's spies slipped down the scarlet thread from the window of Rahab's house and found themselves outside the town wall. Scarcely half a mile away from them rose the vast shadow of the mountains that lie to the back of Jericho; an impenetrable fastness of caves and corries in which men could remain, and have remained, hidden for years.

They slipped away into the shadows of those mountains, and lay hidden somewhere on the slopes of Mount Quarantana until a chance came to run back to Joshua with their news.

Before Jericho was destroyed Joshua fulfilled the promise made by his spies. He sent for Rahab and her family and "left them without the camp of Israel."

Legend, quite naturally, has been busy with the name of Rahab. One rabbinical tradition states that she married Joshua and became the ancestress of seven prophets. But it seems more likely that she married one of the spies! If Rahab of Jericho is the Rahab who married Salmon, son of Nahshon, and begat Boaz, she was an ancestress of the royal line of David.

"With our eyes cast on Rahab the harlot, hope springs in our heart for all the lost and outcast world," says one writer.

When you stand on the mounds of Jericho, which were recently excavated by Professor Garstang, the opening chapters of Joshua seemed unusually vivid. You can see the place at Gilgal, two miles away, where the Israelites camped; at the back rise the barren slopes of the mountain where the spies lay hidden.

Most interesting of all are the remains of the wall of

Jericho, a rampart of mud brick that must have been about twenty or twenty-five feet in height. This had collapsed in a violent manner, as if from earthquake shocks, and had fallen outwards. Certain stretches of it, which are marvellously preserved, have been so twisted that rows of bricks that were once lying flat are lying almost upright.

It is easy to trace the foundations of houses and the line of narrow streets. Near the wall is the ruin of a mud house which is in slightly better preservation than the others. Imagination, of course, likes to claim this as the house of Rahab.

Ruth

OUR EXPERIENCE of life tells us that recorded history is not always the whole story: while nations rise and fall, the little dramas of the human heart go on in secret all the time.

History does not often notice these dramas. History deals in large canvases crowded with struggling figures: it is like a searchlight that, probing in the dark of the past, lights up the march of armies, sweeps over battlefields, strays a moment on a king struggling to maintain his power, or on slaves fighting to be free.

Just now and again, however, the beam of history falls, as if by accident, on a quiet little landscape where the sun is shining and the corn is growing, where men are courteous and noble, and where women are brave and kind of heart. One of these quiet corners of history is the short *Book of Ruth*.

It is one of the most lovely idylls in literature. It has enchanted every age. Ruth and her mother-in-law, Naomi, are among the best-loved women in history, for the fragrance of their devotion has shed itself down the centuries.

The story of Ruth is so well known that one may be criticized for telling it again. But I believe that such stories cannot be told too often.

During a time of famine in Bethlehem, a man and his wife and their two sons decided to leave their native countryside and to live in the Land of Moab. The man was Elimelech, the wife was Naomi, and the two sons were Mahlon and Chilion.

In the Bible such journeys seem to be long and arduous. The men who go "into a far country," or who leave the hills of Judah for the Land of Moab, seem to us, if we have never seen Palestine, to be great travellers.

But Palestine is a small country, no larger, in fact, than Wales, so that one is always surprised that so much could have happened in so small a compass.

The Land of Moab, for instance, which sounds so remote, is the most prominent object visible from Bethlehem. Bethlehem stands on one range of hills and Moab is the range that rises opposite, to the east of the Dead Sea. So when this Bethlehem family decided to emigrate to Moab they made one of those short Biblical journeys of thirty miles or so into a land that was remote, not in mileage, but in mind.

Distances in the Bible are not measured from one place to another, but from God. Naomi and her husband felt that they were going into a far country because Moab was a land of foreign worship.

Misfortune and poverty came their way. The husband died. The sons, who had married Moabite women, died also. Naomi was left alone in a strange land with her two daughters-in-law. One was Ruth; the other was Orpah.

Naomi, destitute and broken-hearted, gazed over the emptiness of the Jordan Valley towards the opposite hills of Judah and decided to return, poor and helpless as she was, to her own people. First she broke to Ruth and Orpah the news that they must return to their families because there would be no welcome for them on the opposite hills. Orpah kissed her and, with tears running down her face, turned back, but Ruth "clave unto her."

She clung to Naomi and gave voice to the most exquisite expression of love and loyalty in the whole of literature:

"Whither thou goest," she cried, "I will go; and where thou lodgest, I will lodge: thy people shall be my people, and thy God my God: where thou diest, will I die, and there will I be buried: the Lord do so to me, and more also, if ought but death part thee and me."

So Naomi and Ruth went on together to Bethlehem; and it was the time of the barley harvest.

Ruth is unique in the history of woman because her story is not primarily that of her love for a man, but of her passionate devotion to a character which modern humour has claimed as its own: her mother-in-law. Only the greatest writer would dare to take this as his theme.

It is an axiom in modern life that a man's mother and his young wife do not always agree. We all know a few brilliant exceptions to this rule, but I cannot think of any literature, other than the *Book of Ruth,* in which this relationship is exalted.

The character of Ruth is intensely interesting. There is nothing to suggest that she was beautiful, as Rebekah and Rachel were beautiful, or that she was competent, as Sarah was competent. Ruth's outstanding quality was a beauty of heart, a generosity of soul, a firm sense of duty, and a meekness which often goes hand in hand with the gift of decision.

[78]

Her desire to follow Naomi into poverty was no sacrifice. She loved the older woman and asked only to be able to help her and to make life easier for her, to work for her and to share her life.

Thus, to my mind, Ruth is not an abnormal character, although she is an unusual one. One must know very little of human nature if one has never met Ruth. But, at the same time, the world does not consider her spectacular or heroic. But the Bible, casting the floodlight of its revelation on her portrait, has placed her among the immortals.

Under the Jewish law the poor were allowed to glean in any harvest field. So Ruth set herself this weary, humble task in order to support the older woman.

The picture of Ruth "in tears amid the alien corn" is an immortal one; and when you stand in Bethlehem it is easy to imagine how she would often gaze across to the Moab Mountains, remembering that among their purple shadows was lived all she had known of happiness.

As Ruth was following the reapers one day, the owner of the field, a man named Boaz, noticed her and asked her name.

"It is the Moabitish damsel that came back with Naomi out of the country of Moab," he was told. The farmer—"a mighty man of wealth" we are told—was related to Naomi's dead husband and was therefore a connection by marriage of Ruth. He looked at her with tender compassion and, because she was a stranger in Judah, he spoke in a kindly, considerate way to her, telling her to make herself at home, promising her that the rude jests of the harvesters should not annoy her, and inviting her at meal times to go among his people and dip her food in the sour wine with the rest.

His attitude was free from all suspicion of self-interest. He was not in love with the young stranger, or, if so, he was not aware of it. There is a certain type of mind that is unwilling to admit disinterested generosity in others, yet surely most of us have at some time encountered such kindness as that which Boaz showed to Ruth.

It is true that he was to fall deeply in love with her, but at that moment his feelings were merely tender and protective.

When she was out of earshot he told the reapers to "let fall some of the handfuls of purpose for her, and leave them that she may glean them, and rebuke her not."

In this little furtive act of kindness, and in the delicacy of the thought, Boaz revealed the true generosity of his mind.

There is perhaps nothing so difficult for us to imagine as an entirely different code of conduct or a standard of morality unlike our own.

In the time of Ruth (before the establishment of Levitical Law) it was the custom of the next of kin of a dead man to purchase, or "redeem," his estate in order to keep it within the tribe. If the man left a young and childless wife, it was the duty of the next of kin to marry her and, by having children, save the family name from extinction.

Therefore, any young widow like Ruth would regard her dead husband's next of kin as her rightful affianced husband. It is absolutely necessary to grasp this strange custom, otherwise the action of Naomi, which Ruth obeyed, must have to our eyes the appearance of a plot to entrap Boaz.

Naomi saw in Boaz the next-of-kin "who should redeem," and she told Ruth that she must place herself under his protection. The time chosen was the night when, after winnowing the barley on the threshing-floor, Boaz would sleep in the barn to prevent thieves from stealing his grain, as the Arabs do to this day:

"Wash thyself therefore, and anoint thee," commanded Naomi, "and put thy raiment upon thee, and get thee down to the floor: but make not thyself known unto the man, until he shall have done eating and drinking. And it shall be, when he lieth down, that thou shalt mark the place where he shall lie, and thou shalt go in, and uncover his feet, and lay thee down; and he will tell thee what thou shalt do."

Ruth replied: "All that thou sayest unto me I will do."

When it was dark, and when Boaz had curled himself up in his robe to sleep, Ruth stole into the barn and lay down at his feet.

"Who art thou?" he asked.

"I am Ruth, thine handmaid," she whispered, "spread therefore thy skirt over thy handmaid, for thou art a near kinsman."

In this way she appealed to the custom of the time, and Boaz praised her for her modesty and her virtue. But he told her that there was a still nearer kinsman. It was this other man's right to redeem Ruth, but, should he be unable to do so, Boaz promised to take over his responsibility.

Ruth lay at his feet all that night, and in the greyness of the morning went back to Naomi. Boaz went to the gate of Bethlehem and, calling the elders round him, transacted the business in a manner which carries us straight into the heart of a forgotten social order.

He called them all to witness that he had bought the property of Naomi's husband and her sons, and that he had purchased Ruth to be his wife "to raise up the name of the dead upon his inheritance."

Ruth and Boaz married and she bore him a son. "And Naomi took the child and placed it in her bosom and became nurse unto it." The child was Obed, who became the father of Jesse, who became the father of David. From the line of David, and in David's town, was born in time, Jesus Christ.

In the soul of Jesus the wedding bells of Ruth and Boaz

are rung once more [wrote Mr. George Matheson]. Here again Moab and Israel meet together. In the heart of the Son of Man the Gentile stands side by side with the Jew as the recipient of a common Divine fatherhood.

Deborah

THE WORD Deborah means "a bee." It is an appropriate
name for the woman who busied herself so tirelessly with
the affairs of Israel and stung the enemies of Jehovah in
battle on the Plain of Armageddon.

Deborah is the first great woman nationalist. It may
seem extraordinary that in Old Testament law women

could be grouped with the household chattels and yet at the same time become, like Deborah, leaders of the nation.

She was, of course, an exceptional woman and she reminds us of Boadicea and of Joan of Arc. She had the fury of the one and the divine conviction of the other.

In the great gallery of Old Testament women she stands for ever as the prototype of those women who, in times when men lack faith and courage, suddenly take the reins of leadership and invite a nation to ride with them to victory.

She had a husband whose name was Lapidoth. We know nothing else about him. He shares the obscurity of all such husbands, but from the fact that he did not, apparently, accompany his fiery wife to the wars, we are at liberty to wonder whether he was the meek and gentle type of man whom such women as Deborah seem inevitably to marry.

In Sir Charles Marston's book, *The Bible Is True*, a summary of modern archaeological discoveries, the date when Deborah lived is given as 1194 to 1154 B.C. Those, say modern scholars, were forty years of peace that she obtained for Israel.

An understanding of what was happening in Palestine at this period is necessary before one can appreciate the story of Deborah. It was a time of frightful anarchy. The Israelites had invaded, but had not conquered more than a portion of, a land which already supported a native civilization. The loosely organized Hebrew tribes settled down and began to learn how to be agriculturists. They had to forsake their tents and huddle together in stone villages. When their crops were bad they wondered whether Jehovah, who had cherished them in the wilderness, had forgotten them now that they were farmers, and so the weaker of faith among them, or perhaps the more earnest agriculturists, began to worship the local Canaanite gods in the hope that they might have better luck. During this time better-armed people, the Canaanites, the Perizzites, the Ammonites, and, later, the pirate Philistines, raided the new settlements.

People nowadays are greatly shocked when they read the Biblical account of the conquest of Canaan [wrote Lewis Browne in *The Story of the Jews*]. When these ancient Hebrews conquered a city they followed the custom of the time and "devoted" it to their god: that is to say, they stole all the gold and silver, butchered all the cattle and human beings, and then burnt the whole place to the ground.

They plundered and pillaged right and left, razed fortresses, and decimated whole tribes. They were like ravenous beasts out of the wilderness! But what else could one expect of them? After all, they were still half-savages. How do our "civilized" nations behave in time of war?

How indeed!

The time of Deborah was therefore a period when

there was no unity in Israel. The people "went awhoring after other gods," "and the anger of the Lord was hot against Israel." It was a time of constant raiding, of murder and highway robbery, so that the old trade routes were deserted, "and the travellers walked through byways."

The man who for twenty years had raided the Israelites with a well-trained army of nine hundred iron chariots was Sisera. The cities trembled behind their walls as he drove his chariots at them. He was apparently invincible.

Deborah dwelt in the south under the palm-tree between Ramch and Bethel. Although there had been prophetesses before, such as Miriam, the sister of Moses, there had been no woman quite like Deborah. "The people of Israel came up to her for judgment."

No hereditary authority marked her out for distinction. She was not a queen like Jezebel or Athaliah. She was an ordinary woman who was chosen by the people to become their leader.

One imagines that her influence spread through the dispirited tribes much as that of Boadicea spread from mouth to mouth through Roman Britain. Her outstanding personality, her faith in the future, her inspiring contempt for weakness and inaction and, above all, her belief in God, made her the uncrowned queen of the Children of Israel.

She summoned the one man in that feeble age who

seemed to her capable of leadership. This was Barak of Kedesh-Naphtali. Although Barak had a divine command to gather his army on Mount Tabor and rout the chariots of Sisera, it has been truly said that he was the kind of man who finds it easier to believe in a woman than in God.

If thou wilt go with me, then I will go: but if thou wilt not go with me, then I will not go.

That was Barak's reply to Deborah when she called on him to make war on Sisera.

True, it was an admission of weakness, but it was also a mighty compliment to the mentality and the influence of Deborah. One does not feel that Barak was a coward: one realizes that he was in the presence of an overwhelming personality.

"I will surely go with thee," replied Deborah, adding, with a touch of womanly scorn, that "the Lord shall sell Sisera into the hand of a woman."

Mount Tabor is a high, saddle-backed hill standing by itself to the south of Nazareth. From the top of it you look down on a low flat plain twenty miles in extent and bounded to the south by the blue hills of Samaria.

This is the Plain of Armageddon, the ancient meeting-place of the Eastern and the Western empires. Every army that has ever fought in Palestine has marched across this plain, from the forces of Deborah and Saul to those of Napoleon and Allenby.

It was on this plain that Deborah's infantry marched towards the cloud of Canaanite chariots led by Sisera. At the critical moment a semi-tropical downpour, which sometimes occurs in this country, came driving into the faces of the Canaanites. They lashed their chariots onward in the storm of sleet and rain, but with every step the horses plunged into a deeper mire that clogged the chariot wheels.

"The stars in their courses fought against Sisera."

The united Israelites routed the enemy. Sisera fled on foot to meet a terrible death in the tent of a nomad woman, "and the land had rest forty years."

The account of this battle in the sixth chapter of *Judges,* which is known as the *Song of Deborah,* is one of the most remarkable descriptions in the Old Testament. It is a flaming song of triumph, which scholars agree was written, if not by Deborah herself, by some one who lived in the time of her victory.

Some have called this song one of the most savage battle-cries ever written—a poem bristling with sword-points—and others have heard in it the voice of Good triumphing over Evil.

It is notable that so fierce an ode should rise at its end to such lofty heights: "So let all Thine enemies perish, O Lord," cries Deborah. "But let them that love Him be as the sun when he goeth forth in his might."

That is the key to Deborah's character. It is the character of a woman who, like Joan of Arc, buckled on the armour of a man because she heard voices commanding her to action.

Delilah

IT IS not known whether Delilah was an Israelite or a
Philistine. One assumes, however, because her birthplace
was at Sorek—at that time in Philistine territory—and
from the ease with which the Philistines bribed her to
betray Samson, that she belonged to the enemy people.

She was the type of woman created from the beginning

of time to be the downfall of men like Samson. She is the classic instance of the truth that, if a man is given to philandering, the time will probably come when he will encounter a Delilah who will betray him into the hands of his enemies.

The police reports are always telling the old story of Samson and Delilah. It comes up in a number of ingenious disguises, a theme capable of infinite variation, but the main motif throughout is that of a man who plunges deeper and deeper into his own lack of self-control until the moment arrives when, trapped and shorn of his strength, he is blinded and bound.

Thousands of people who go to the cinema see this story without recognizing it. Writers of fiction have been dressing it up in various guises for centuries.

Commentators on Bible women generally leave out Delilah because Samson was such a thorn in the path of the old-fashioned Bible critic.

In spite of the uplifting grandeur of Milton's conception of this story, and despite the many attempts of the theologian to purify the life of Samson by regarding it as an allegory, the student of Hebrew literature knows perfectly well that the history of Samson is a remarkable intrusion of a popular legend into the spiritual record of a people. It has the same hearty, but incongruous air that the drinking scene from *Twelfth Night* would have if, through an accident in a printer's office, it became bound up in St. Augustine's *Confessions*.

Like all stories which have come from the common people, it has a reality and an earthly gusto of its own. Samson is more like Rob Roy and Burns than he is like the mighty prophets and leaders of Israel. He is a frolicsome giant, a man swept by mighty gusts of laughter, and a great practical joker. This extraordinary character seems in the strangest way to link the common folk of Israel thousands of years ago with the English people of, say, Shakespeare's time.

There is something rather Falstaffian about Samson as he plays his jokes on the Philistines, asks them riddles, slays them contemptuously with the jawbone of an ass, ties torches to the tails of foxes and chases them into the Philistine corn, strides love-making into Philistine cities and escapes with the gates upon his bull-like shoulders. Sir James Frazer has called him

that roystering swashbuckler . . . His talent would seem to have lain rather in the direction of brawling and fighting, burning down people's corn ricks, and beating up the quarters of loose women; in short, he appears to have shone in the character of a libertine and a rake-hell rather than in a strictly judicial capacity.

With the appearance of Delilah, however, Samson becomes a tragedy. The story of his betrayal and fall is one of the most graphic and pitiful in the Bible.

There is heartrending tragedy in the spectacle of that once light-hearted giant, helpless and blind, grinding the Philistine wheat in the prison at Gaza, and one must, I think, have a cruel heart to feel that this hideous fate was a just retribution.

Samson, like all such characters, had redeeming qualities, although even the most sympathetic and reverent critics agree that he failed to live up to his possibilities. He was one of those men who are always promising to turn over a new leaf only to find that their physical appetites are greater than their sense of rectitude.

Delilah was the last of a series of Philistine women with whom Samson fell in love. An apologist might argue that she was a Philistine heroine—a Judith—who betrayed Samson for the sake of her people. But is there sufficient evidence? There is surely more evidence that Delilah was that not uncommon character: the woman who would betray any man for money.

The chapter which describes Delilah begins significantly with: "Then went Samson to Gaza, and saw there an harlot, and went in unto her."

This woman was not Delilah. But the mention of her casts a light on the habits of Samson. Immediately we learn that:

And it came to pass afterward that he loved a woman in the valley of Sorek, whose name was Delilah. And the lords of the Philistines came up unto her, and said unto her, entice him, and see wherein his great strength lieth, and by what means we may prevail against him, that we may bind him to afflict him; and we will give thee every one of us eleven hundred pieces of silver.

If Delilah had been a woman like Judith, willing, no matter how hateful her task, to betray a man for the sake of her nation, why should they have put a price on her betrayal?

The bribe proves that Delilah betrayed Samson for money. She was that hateful character who under the guise of love winds her way into the confidence of a man, learns his secrets and sells them to his enemies; and the lords of the Philistines had no illusions about her.

No one can read the vivid story of Samson's fall, however, without the knowledge that he also had no illusions about Delilah. He knew that she was a worthless traitor, but he was so confident of himself that he did not fear her.

"And Delilah said to Samson, Tell me, I pray thee, wherein thy great strength lieth."

If Samson had been in doubt about the intentions of Delilah he would not have told her three lies, and three such humorous lies. He was playing with her in his characteristically clumsy way, knowing, perhaps, that her Philistine friends were all the time hidden behind the curtain.

We must imagine that her constant questioning occurred over a period of time. On each occasion Samson put her off and beat the Philistines who rushed in to overcome him.

At length, "when she pressed him daily with her words, and urged him, so that his soul was vexed unto death," he told her the truth—a belief common in antiquity— that his strength resided in the hair of his head, the un-shorn locks of a Nazarite.

The lords of the Philistines came up unto her and brought money in their hand. And she made him sleep upon her knees; and she called for a man, and she caused him to shave off the seven locks of his head; and she began to afflict him, and his strength went from him.

Poor Samson awakened from his drugged sleep con-fident, as usual, that he was a giant in a pigmy world, but "he wist not that the Lord was departed from him."

The Philistines took him and put out his eyes. They carried him to Gaza and bound him with fetters of brass. And in the prison house they harnessed the blind giant to the grinding-mill.

The one touch of sublimity is his death. He is called from prison as a kind of buffoon to "make sport" for the Philistines at the feast of their god Dagon. He hears their mockery and, like an echo of the past, comes the memory of his destiny and the thought of what he might have been. His youth and his strength seem to return to him.

He calls on God to help him.

Tragic, and no longer undignified, the blind giant grasps the pillars of the hall and, with the cry, "Let me die with the Philistines," brings down an appalling avalanche on his tormentors.

Delilah vanished, as such women do, when her task was completed. She had played her part and had received her reward.

I was reminded of her the other day when I was talking to a criminal lawyer. I asked him how it was that the prosecution in a recent case managed to bring certain charges against a ruined man.

"It was simple," he said. "A girl pretended to be in love with him and gave him away."

"You mean they bribed her?"

"Of course," he said.

The Witch of Endor

"WHAT IS your idea of the Witch of Endor?" an artist once asked me.

"Have you ever been to a spiritualist seance?" I replied.

"Yes."

"And what did the medium look like?"

"She was a very ordinary woman."

"That is my idea of the Witch of Endor."

"I agree with you," he replied. "You know, of course, that every artist who has ever drawn the Witch of Endor has pictured her like one of Macbeth's witches: an old, smoke-dried hag, toothless and with white hair, crouching over a fire while spirits hover in the air and bats fly round about. That is the conventional picture."

"I know it is. But I prefer to imagine a Witch of Endor who might have had a 'familiar spirit' in South Norwood."

To the east of the flat green plain of Esdraelon, or Armageddon, is a slight hill on whose slopes is a poverty-stricken Arab village called to this day Endur. There are a few stone huts and caves, from one of which a thin stream of water flows into a narrow canal that guides it through the gardens.

Old grain pits, tombs in the rocks and ancient water cisterns prove that the history of this village goes back into the mists of time.

En-dor means the spring of Dor, or of the Dwelling. The stream of water that still trickles from the cave is the same stream that ran there in the time of Saul and gave its name to the place where the Witch of Endor lived.

The scene in which Saul seeks the help of this medium is intensely dramatic. The desperate king, conscious that the Divine approval has departed from him, terrified by the powers massed against him and conscious also, perhaps, of his approaching death, gropes in the darkness of his soul for some comfort.

He cannot pray. He has therefore ceased to hope. His enemies, the Philistines, are camped about him on the Plain of Esdraelon, while he, with the Israelite forces, commands the rising ground at Mount Giboa.

"When Saul saw the hosts of the Philistines he was afraid and his heart trembled greatly," we are told, and "when Saul inquired of the Lord, the Lord answered him not."

Saul sinks into melancholy and despair. He thinks of the great Samuel and wishes that he were alive so that he might go to him for comfort. But Samuel is dead. The tortured man then, with the superstition of a witch-hunter, resolves to break the rules of his life and consult a medium.

It was against the Law of Moses to do this.

There shall not be found with thee [runs the Law] any one that useth divination, one that practiseth augury, or an enchanter, or a sorcerer, or a charmer, or a consulter with a familiar spirit, or a wizard, or a necromancer. For whatsoever doeth these things is an abomination to Jehovah.

Saul himself had driven out the spiritualists and the mediums from Israel: he had "put away those that had familiar spirits and the wizards out of the land." Now, in his extremity, he turns to those whom he has persecuted:

"Seek me a woman that hath a familiar spirit!" he commands.

His servants answer him:

"Behold there is a woman that hath a familiar spirit at En-dor."

In the darkness of the night—the night before the battle that destroyed him and his royal house—Saul, disguised in a long cloak and accompanied by only two attendants, climbs the slight volcanic hill to the dwelling of the wise woman of En-dor.

It has been well said that the power and the sombre tragedy of this story hold the reader spellbound. Death is in the air. A man with only a few hours to live is about to question the spirits of the dead.

The Witch of Endor receives her mysterious visitors with the caution of all persecuted seers and fortune-tellers. Perhaps the scene becomes more vivid, certainly more modern, in Dr. Moffatt's *New Translation of the Bible*.

"Inquire for me as a medium," Saul commands her, "bring me up the ghost of someone whom I name to you."

The medium replies:

"You know what Saul has done, cutting mediums and

wizards out of the country! Why, then, are you laying a trap for my life, to have me put to death?"

But the pitiful earnestness of the disguised king conquers her fear of prosecution.

"Whom shall I bring up for you?" she asks.

"Bring up Samuel," whispers Saul.

The woman looks at him.

"Why have you deceived me?" she asks. "You *are* Saul!"

"Have no fear," he cried. "What do you see?"

"I see a god coming out of the earth."

"What is he like?"

"It is an old man coming up; he is covered with a mantle."

"So Saul knew it was Samuel; he bowed with his face to the ground and did obeisance."

Certainly no spiritualist, and no one who has ever attended a successful seance, will doubt the lifelike truth of the above dialogue. It is the sort of conversation that goes on in the dark to-day as it went on in the dark of the little hill-top on the night before the Philistines drove Saul to his death. The commentators of the nineteenth century were forced by the educated opinion of their age to treat this incident as hallucination, or as a piece of elaborate trickery devised by the Witch of Endor.

It is obvious to any one to-day that the Witch of Endor

was not a pantomime witch or a hag out of *Macbeth:* she was just an ordinary medium.

Whether the spirit which she saw was really Samuel or not, the fact remains that the phenomena reported during this seance were the same as those which are known to modern spiritualists.

The Voice spoke to Saul, probably through the medium, and Saul was convinced that he was speaking to the man whom he had once known so well.

The Voice gave him no hope. It foretold instead his death on the following day. The spirit, after rebuking the trembling Saul, spoke these words:

"To-morrow shalt thou and thy sons be with me."

Saul fell senseless on the earth.

The interesting thing about the Witch of Endor is that the Bible narrator has not drawn her with a broomstick or with a stuffed crocodile or with a corps of tame bats. All those trappings came in during the Middle Ages.

She is painted not only as an ordinary woman but as a kindhearted and compassionate one. Her portrait is extraordinarily complete.

And the woman came unto Saul and saw that he was sore troubled, and said unto him, Behold thy handmaid hath obeyed thy voice, and I have put my life in my hand . . . now, therefore, hearken thou also unto the voice of thy handmaid, and let me set a morsel of bread before thee; and eat that thou mayest have strength when thou goest on thy way.

In other words she made a very human speech. She said:

"I have obeyed you. I have risked prosecution. Even death. You have listened to the voice of Samuel: now listen to my voice. You must eat something."

The terrified king refused to eat, but the kindhearted "witch" insisted on mothering him.

And the woman had a fat calf in the house; and she hasted and killed it, and took flour and kneaded it and did bake unleavened bread thereof. And she brought it before Saul, and before his servants; and they did eat. Then they rose up and went away that night.

On the next day Saul and his three sons met death, and his army was scattered.

I think that the Witch of Endor is a most attractive character. When one visualizes her, not as the witch in a fairy tale, but as a real woman who believed herself to be, and convinced others that she was in touch with an unseen world, one realizes how very life-like she is.

Once her seance was over, she became anxious only to comfort and take care of the stricken Saul. She knew that he would be lying dead on the plain before the sun had set on the following day. He could not hurt her. He was unable to punish her for breaking the law, as he had commanded her to do. Her one thought was to heal his body and to give him strength to go out and meet his fate.

Therefore, I claim that the Witch of Endor is one of the most attractive exponents of "the Black Art" in early literature.

Michal

IT HAS been said, rather cruelly, that in any love affair it is often difficult to know who is the hunter and who the hunted.

A peculiarly feminine quality is the gift of pretending to fly while really in pursuit, or perhaps it would be better to say that history records many a love story which would suggest that flight may be the most deadly form of chase.

Schopenhauer, and other woman-haters, have laid it down, with the dogmatism of bachelors, that woman is always the hunter and man always the hunted, but less prejudiced observers will not, perhaps, agree.

The first woman in the Bible, however, who took the initiative in a love affair was Michal, the first wife of David. She was the second daughter of that haunted and God-forsaken man, King Saul.

All the women whose lives we have so far examined have observed an Oriental submission towards their wooers, no matter how they have developed in later life. Alone among them, Michal seems to have singled out David as her husband long before he had any such ideas, and to have persisted in her love for him while he was engaged to be married to her elder sister, Merab.

She cherished a romantic passion for David. We can, in fact, regard her as the first female hero-worshipper, the remote predecessor of all those ardent young women who frame the photographs of film actors whom they have never met. Nothing could be farther apart from her attitude than that, say, of Rebekah, who meeting a stranger at the village well, unquestioningly accepted the engagement ring of an Isaac whom she had never seen.

Michal, on the other hand, marked down the unsuspect-

ing hero and said to herself: "I am going to marry that
man."

We have a more detailed and intimate knowledge of
David than of any hero of antiquity, not excepting Julius
Caesar. His portrait has been etched with an inspired
pen. There is nothing to add to it.

He came to the court of Saul as a young hero—"a
mighty man of valour"—and a skilful musician, a combi-
nation of qualities that has been found throughout history irresistible in the courts of love.

When an evil spirit brooded over Saul, inducing moods
of the deepest melancholy, young David, who like the
Arab shepherd boy to-day had learnt his music among
the sheepfolds on the hills, was called with his harp to
charm the king's spirit back into the light.

One can imagine that at such moments Michal, drawing aside a purple hanging, would gaze on the splendid
young man who, bent above his harp, plucked beauty out
of the sombre air round the throne of Saul.

David had already vanquished the heart of Jonathan,
and their friendship is one of the most beautiful in literature. Michal was conquered by him, too. The whole
court of Saul, in fact, turned to the young shepherd as
though in prophetic welcome to the lad born to be king.

Saul alone hated him. He was jealous and frightened.
As David grew and progressed, the heart of Saul grew

blacker towards him with the hate that a man deserted by God can direct on the upright and the good.

With evil cunning, Saul promised the hand of his elder daughter, Merab, to the young warrior when he had distinguished himself in war with the Philistines. He hoped, by an invitation to the very steps of the throne, to make the young man reckless in battle and so bring about his death.

Therefore Michal was forced to endure the spectacle of the man she loved fighting to win her sister.

The sorrow of a girl who is in love with her sister's betrothed is not, unfortunately, rare in life or in fiction; but Michal was more fortunate than some sisters because David was not in love with Merab. He seems to have plunged into the national pastime of slaughtering the Philistines with the desire rather, as he thought, to please Saul than to win a bride.

When Saul cheated him and married Merab to Adriel, the Meholathite, there is no indication that David minded very much. Michal, on the other hand, knew that her chance had come.

It was whispered to Saul that his younger daughter Michal was in love with David, "and the thing pleased him." He decided to foster the love affair that she might be a "snare" for him, never doubting that his paternal influence with her would be greater than her love for David.

Therefore he proposed, as David was a poor man and could not pay the large sum which kings usually demanded for their daughters, that he would accept, instead, the slaying of one hundred Philistines.

This task presented no difficulty to David, who went out and slew two hundred; and Saul, enraged to see the young man return alive, was, nevertheless, forced to give Michal to him.

After marriage it is clear that Michal captivated the heart of David. She was entirely devoted to him. They present a perfect picture of domestic bliss. Saul, however, continued to plot against his son-in-law. Every military success of David's was sufficient to fling the king into an insane passion.

One day, when David was playing the harp in the palace, Saul rose up and flung a javelin at him, but the young man dodged and fled to his house while the spear was still quivering in the wall.

He told Michal of the king's madness and, while they discussed the danger, the house was surrounded by spies waiting for a chance either to slay or to capture David.

Michal said to her husband: "If thou save not thy life to-night, to-morrow thou shalt be slain."

Tradition says that it was upon this night, while assassins lurked in every shadow, that David composed Psalm lix.:

Deliver me from mine enemies, O my God:
Defend me from them that rise up against me.
Deliver me from the workers of iniquity, and save me
from bloody men.
For, lo, they lie in wait for my soul: the mighty are gath-
ered against me;
Not for my transgression, nor for my sin, O Lord. . . .

As the assassins crept nearer, Michal's quick brain
devised a plan of action. First, she let David down from
the window on a cord, just as Rahab let down the spies
from the walls of Jericho.

He vanished into the darkness; and so began his years
of wandering. Then, like many a brave woman who
has helped a man to escape, she plotted to gain time.
She took the "teraphim," or household god, and placed
it in David's bed, covering it with bedclothes and plac-
ing its head on a pillow of goat's hair.

From this incident it has been assumed that these
mysterious images, of which very little is known, were
sometimes life-size.

When the assassins broke in, Michal pointed to the
bed and told them that her lord was ill. They, probably
glad of an excuse, sped back to Saul with the news. But
he commanded them to bring the sick man to him on
the bed.

It was then that Michal's deception was discovered.
The mad king stormed against her, but she lied to him,

telling him that David had threatened to kill her unless she allowed him to escape.

Thus Michal first appears in the Bible as a lovesick young girl, a devoted wife and one of those brave women, like Flora Macdonald and Lady Nithsdale, who with nerve and ingenuity have snatched men from the executioner. Her second appearance, however, shows us a changed woman.

Years passed. David and Michal did not meet. She was at her father's court; he was the romantic fly-by-night, hiding in caves, gathering his troops and planning the day when he should gain the throne of Israel.

The characters in the Bible are, even the greatest of them, not perfect people. Therein lies their fascination. Their faults are our faults.

How untrue to fairy-tales, but how true to life it is that during their separation Michal and David should have forgotten each other. David married another woman, Abigail, and Michal was married by Saul to Phalti.

The time came when Saul lay on Gilboa with his own sword in his stomach and the Philistine arrows in his body; and the northern tribes wanted to make peace with David. His terms were that Michal should be restored to him.

Had he really forgotten? Some may say that he loved her, as men do, all the time, hiding her image in his heart; others may say that he wanted Saul's daughter in order to strengthen his claim to Saul's throne. How can we possibly know?

Michal was, therefore, torn from her devoted husband, Phalti, who "went with her, weeping as he went," and once more David, now a mighty man, met his first wife. But she had changed. Perhaps he had changed too.

On the day when David brought the Ark of the Covenant, the sacred symbol of Jehovah's presence among his people, from its temporary resting-place into the city of Jerusalem, Michal watched her husband from the window, and what did she see? She saw, as you can see to-day in the sacred Arab processions of Nebi Musa, the great king whirling and dancing before the Ark of God.

It was the greatest religious moment of his life. His feelings transcended speech. His heart overflowed. Therefore he danced. But "Michal, Saul's daughter, looked through a window, and saw King David leaping and dancing before the Lord; and *she despised him in her heart.*"

One could write so much about Michal: she worshipped him when he was poor and unknown and now that he was king "she despised him in her heart." She met him and cried ironically:

"How glorious was the king of Israel to-day, who uncovered himself to-day in the eyes of the handmaids of

his servants, as one of the vain fellows shamelessly un-
covereth himself!"

David looked at her with the knowledge that they
could never understand each other. He told her that
what he had done was not for human eyes but for the
eyes of God.

David never forgave her and she disappears from history. He realized that they could never love the same
God. Therefore he cut her from his heart.

Abigail

THE REMARKABLE thing about the women of the Bible is that such complete portraits have been drawn in so few words. They are like the miniature portraits of the eighteenth century, whose full beauty and detail can be seen only with the help of a magnifying-glass.

The glass we must use on these Bible portraits is that

of the imagination. Only by our knowledge, love, and sympathy for our fellow men and women can we expand them into large-size pictures.

A perfect gem in miniature is the story of Abigail. She also increases the scope of the portraits: she is the good woman who is married to a drunkard and a boor.

When you travel from Hebron towards the southern desert of Palestine, you suddenly leave the desolate brown limestone hills, the bare little valleys and the dry watercourses and come with surprise to a plateau about nine miles by three, which might be a bit of Aberdeenshire.

The ground is free from stones, the barley and the wheat shine in the sun, and above the plateau rise several mounds whose ruins hold all that is left of Maon, Ziph, and Carmel.

This is where Nabal and his wife, Abigail, lived when David was an outlaw in the surrounding desert. On the fat land Nabal grazed his three thousand sheep and his herd of a thousand goats.

The future King of Israel at this romantic period of his life, hiding from Saul and gathering his supporters in caves and deserts, reminds us of Bonnie Prince Charlie and also of Rob Roy. He and his merry men lived by levying a kind of tax on the sheep farmers of the fertile plateau.

In return for protection against the lawless Bedouin, the farmers were only too willing to pay the outlaws so much grain at harvest time or so much wool at shearing. It paid the farmers to have David as a friend rather than an enemy; those who refused his protection found independence expensive.

When David heard that Nabal was sheep-shearing, he sent ten young men to remind him, in a polite but pointed manner, that during the past season no hurt had come to his shepherds and his sheep.

"Give, I pray thee, whatsoever cometh to thine hand unto thy servants," concluded the messengers. In other words, "We have looked after you for a year. What was it worth to you?"

Nabal was a coarse-grained drunkard. It is a remarkable fact that there are few instances of impoliteness in the Old Testament. Nabal's reply is one of them, for drink coarsens a man's nature and degrades his manners.

"Who is David?" asked Nabal bluntly. It was a deliberately rude and provocative question. We, who make allowances for rudeness and are not bound in the rigid code of Eastern politeness, cannot quite understand how insulting it was.

When David heard of it he simply said, "Gird ye on every man his sword." And they set off to slay Nabal.

Abigail, Nabal's wife, heard of the incident, and, like the wife of many a drunkard, took immediate steps to undo her husband's mistake. How sadly true to life it is that she kept her plan secret from Nabal. She knew well that the blustering, pig-headed fellow would have forbidden her to carry out the action that eventually saved his life.

Marshalling her household, she loaded asses with two hundred loaves, five sheep ready dressed, two skins of wine, two hundred fig-cakes and a load of raisins, and with this peace-offering she set off to meet the angry David.

The meeting of these two is one of the most charming incidents in the Old Testament: David, the future king, hungry, down-at-heels, proud and very splendid; Abigail, gentle, feminine, clever, and—as the Bible tells us—"a woman of good understanding, and of a beautiful countenance."

And when Abigail saw David, she hasted, and lighted off the ass, and fell before David on her face and bowed herself to the ground, and fell at his feet, and said: Upon me, my lord, upon me, let this iniquity be.

David looked at this clever, beautiful woman, and he must have wondered, as many men in the same position have wondered, how such a woman could have married a man like Nabal.

Abigail's generosity, her anxiety to protect a worthless husband, her fine sense of David's qualities, her appeal to the gentler side of him, the keen insight which told her that one day this outlaw would be king over Israel, cooled his anger and recalled him to himself.

One can almost hear the swords going back into their sheaths as David, looking at Abigail, one may be sure with great tenderness, said:

Blessed be the Lord God of Israel, which sent thee this day to meet me: and blessed be thy advice, and blessed be thou, which has kept me from coming to shed blood, and from avenging myself with mine own hand. . . . Go up in peace to thine house.

I think that is one of the most exquisite little cameos in the Bible. David watched Abigail go away from him back towards her boorish husband, knowing well that he had met a woman whom he could love. He turned thoughtfully and rode with his warriors into the brown hills.

When Abigail reached home, her husband was drunk. "He held a feast in his house like the feast of a king; and Nabal's heart was merry within him, for he was very drunken."

The life of a drunkard's wife is full of eloquent silences. Abigail looked at him and said nothing. She knew that to tell him "until the morning light" that she had saved his life and his property would bring down only a storm of abuse and fury.

So she, with the secret in her heart and the memory

of David's chivalrous and suddenly gentle eyes in her mind, sat there and watched her husband become more loathsome in his cups.

In the morning, "when the wine was gone out of Nabal," she told him. One has the impression that he had a seizure, as drunkards often do in moments of sudden passion, or an attack of apoplexy, for "his heart died within him, and he became as a stone."

Possibly his attack was brought on by anger at the loss of his goods, or he was furious with his wife for presuming to meddle in his affairs; or perhaps he was stubbornly enraged to think that David had—as a man of his type would put it to-day—"got the better of him."

The stroke, however, was fatal. "And it came to pass about ten days after, that the Lord smote Nabal, that he died." When David heard the news, he said: "The Lord hath returned the wickedness of Nabal upon his own head."

Abigail had made a deep impression on David. She had gentleness, beauty, piety and, like most women who are married to men like Nabal, she had outstanding tact. David sent an embassy to ask Abigail to become his wife.

As I have said at least once in the course of these pages the matrimonial and extra-marital affairs of the

ABIGAIL

Old Testament heroes are difficult to understand because they belong to an age, a country, and a moral
atmosphere utterly different from ours. David was, of
course, already married to Michal, Saul's daughter. As
we have seen, she had helped him to escape when her
father's spies were seeking him; but he was not to see
her again until the eve of his triumph, and it is perfectly clear that he still felt for her, perhaps love, or
perhaps the romantic attachment that thrives on nothing so much as on absence and memories. In spite of
this there was nothing in the moral code of the time
to prevent him from taking Abigail as his wife. She
received his proposal of marriage with evident joy, for
"she hasted, and arose, and rode upon an ass" and went
straight to David and became his wife.

Unfortunately for the modern taste in romance, David
at the same time had a double wedding, for we learn
that "David also took Ahinoam of Jezreel; and they
were also both of them his wives."

These two women followed the great hero faithfully,
sharing his failures and his triumphs. On one occasion
they were captured by a raiding party of Amalekites,
but David pursued his enemies "and smote them from
the twilight even unto the evening of the next day."

Abigail was with David at Hebron, where she gave
birth to a son called Daniel, of whom nothing further
is known, and no doubt she saw and shared the rise to

power of the man whom she had met as an outlaw on the green uplands of Maon.

We see her very clearly as the wife of the drunkard, Nabal, but we cannot follow her into the mystery of David's harem. We can only hope that a woman of such character and tact, whose name is a synonym for fidelity and loving service, found the happiness she deserved.

The Queen of Sheba

THE JOURNEY of the Queen of Sheba to the Court of
Solomon is one of the most romantic visits in history.
Her name is not given in the Bible, but Arab writers
call her Balkis, and Ethiopian writers call her Makeda.

She was a woman of enterprise, culture, and wealth.
Two countries claim her. She is said to have come

from Saba, or Sabaea, in south-west Arabia, and the Abyssinians not only claim her as their queen, but also trace the descent of their present exiled King from a son who, their legends say, was born by her to Solomon.

So dense, however, is the golden haze of romance around her that the historian is blinded in his attempt to see the Queen of Sheba. Poems, legends, and romances crowd about her memory, some of them wildly fantastic, so that, although she lived in the clear light of history a thousand years before Christ (which to modern archaeologists does not seem very remote), she remains a more legendary character than those far more distant women—Sarah, Rachel, and Rebekah.

The Ethiopian legends tell us that she was inspired to visit Solomon by stories carried to her by the leader of her trade caravans, a merchant named Tamrin.

The fame of Solomon spread rapidly in this way throughout the East. He was the first man to see the commercial possibilities of Arabia and to realize the fabulous riches that lay waiting for any man who could organize the trade of the early world.

The hundreds of caravans that brought wealth to him took back stories of his grandeur and of his wisdom. Nothing appeals so much to the Eastern mind as extravagance and splendour, and Solomon practised both.

He built the first great trading fleet, manned by Phoenician sailors (for the Jews have never loved the sea), and this armada went venturing to the mysterious confines of Ophir, which by some is said to have been India.

If I were writing a book about Solomon I would paint him not as we commonly imagine him, a kind, wise, and pious ruler, but as a greedy and relentless autocrat who by his insatiable love for splendour sucked his people dry, overtaxed them, carried them at one bound from the simple, tribal civilization of his father, David, to the misery of a highly organized commercial state with its ghastly extremes of wealth and poverty.

That is the truth about Solomon. And the proof of it is the revolution that occurred at his death when Israel split up into a Northern and a Southern kingdom.

Saul and David were simple Arab warriors riding over the desert with their armies. Solomon was the mighty Eastern despot with his settled capital, with thousands of slaves building his palaces, hundreds of wives in his harem, merchants sweeping the seas and scouring the deserts to bring back gold to swell his revenue.

A vivid idea of Solomon's income and extravagance is to be found in Professor John Garstang's book *The Heritage of Solomon,* which is a brilliant account of the sociology of ancient Palestine.

The author believes that Solomon's fleets certainly

went as far as India, in search of gold, and probably to Australasia.

Though Solomon was the first great capitalist, he had fine qualities of the mind and a spirituality that, it is true, broke down at last undermined by greed, success, and luxury.

It was to the much advertised wisdom of Solomon, however, that the Queen of Sheba appealed. She "heard of the fame of Solomon concerning the name of the Lord," and she determined to go and "prove him with hard questions."

In other words, Solomon had the reputation of solving theological enigmas, a common occupation in the East, and the Queen of Sheba wished to put to him certain problems about the mystery of life.

Her brief portrait in the Bible is full of charm. She is the rich woman who realizes the emptiness of a life without knowledge, who travels from the ends of the earth to satisfy a hunger for truth.

Among the many legends about her is the strange one that she had never married because of a physical deformity which made her exceedingly sensitive: one of her feet was hairy and formed like that of a goat. Solomon had heard this story, and wishing to find out if it were true, devised a truly Solomonic ruse.

He caused a stream of water to be trained across his throne room so that, as the Queen approached him, she would be forced to lift her skirts and expose her feet.

When the day came, Solomon, seated on his throne surrounded by his great officers of state and all his brilliant court, watched the lovely Queen of the South approaching, and, when she came to the water, she hesitated a moment, then, lifting her skirts, stepped in.

During that second Solomon saw one perfect foot and one deformed foot; but when the Queen of Sheba came through the water towards the throne, both feet were perfect because she had stepped without realizing it, on a piece of wood from Paradise.

I think that perhaps the most interesting of all the legends about Solomon and the Queen of Sheba is one contained in the *Kebra Negast,* the sacred books of Abyssinia, which were translated by the late Sir E. A. Wallis Budge, under the title, *The Queen of Sheba and Her Son Menyelek.* It is as follows:

And as Solomon was talking in this wise with the Queen, he saw a certain labourer carrying a stone upon his head and a skin of water upon his back and shoulders, and his food and his sandals were tied about his loins, and there were pieces of wood in his hands; his garments were ragged and tattered, the sweat fell in drops from his face, and water from the skin of water dripped down upon his feet.

And the labourer passed before Solomon, and as he was going by the King said unto him, "Stand still"; and the labourer stood still. And the King turned to the Queen, and

[131]

said unto her: "Look at this man. Wherein am I superior to this man? And in what am I better than this man? For I am a man of dust and ashes, who to-morrow will become worms and corruption, and yet at this moment I appear like one who will never die. . . . As his death is, so is my death; and as is his life, so is my life.

And he spake further unto the Queen, saying, "What is the use of us, the children of men, if we do not exercise kindness and love upon earth? Are we not all nothingness, mere grass of the field, which withereth in its season and is burnt in the fire? On the earth we provide ourselves with dainty meats, and we wear costly apparel, but even whilst we are alive we are stinking corruption; we provide ourselves with sweet scents and delicate unguents, but even whilst we are alive we are dead in sins and in transgressions. Blessed is the man who knoweth wisdom, that is to say compassion and the fear of God."

When Solomon had spoken much in this way, the Queen of Sheba said to him:

"How thy voice doth please me. And how greatly do thy words and the utterance of thy mouth delight me."

If this was the wisdom which Solomon imparted to the Queen of Sheba it has a strange foretaste of Christianity. It expresses with great beauty and at length what Jesus said in one sentence: "Love the Lord with all thy heart, and with all thy soul, and thy neighbour as thyself."

But Solomon did not, unfortunately, exhibit in his life the compassion and the love for his fellow men expressed by the *Kebra Negast,* so that we are forced to wonder who the unknown scribe was who placed in his mouth sentiments so far in advance of his age.

For three months, the story goes, the lovely Queen of the South listened to the wisdom of Solomon and then "turned and went to her own country."

As the long files of her camels and her dromedaries stand for a moment on the horizon of history we are grateful to her for her brief appearance in the *Book of Kings.*

Gracious, beautiful, powerful, she stands for the hunger that lies in the hearts of kings, as in the hearts of common men, and she represents also the obligation which rests upon all of us, rich and poor, to seek out knowledge and to learn a little wisdom before we, too, turn and go the way of all flesh.

Jezebel

THE MUCH-VAUNTED glory of Solomon was built up on
the slavery and the taxation of his people. Dean Stanley has truly said that he remains the supreme instance
in Sacred History of that which meets us so often in
common history—the union of genius and crime.

Solomon's exactions and his despotism brought to a

head a sense of social injustice and a violent class war-
fare that had been seething throughout his reign.

No sooner was he dead than the threatened revolution occurred. The northern tribes broke away, forming the Kingdom of Israel with its capital in Samaria;
Judah, with its capital at Jerusalem, remained true to
the House of David.

Much of the interest and the drama of the Old Testament is thenceforward centred on the new state. Jerusalem retires for a time into the background, and the
limelight of history falls on the brown hills of Samaria,
where a tremendous social upheaval worked itself out
in terms of religion.

The reader of the Bible is often pained by the fa-
cility with which the Chosen People worshipped false
gods.

Why did they do this? The reason is simple. When
the Children of Israel came in from the desert they
were nomads with a firm faith in Jehovah, but they
invaded an agricultural country and, settling down on
the land, began to learn the Canaanite arts of farming
and village life.

The gods of the Canaanites were nature gods. Every
hill-top had its deities. If rain held off or if the crops
failed, the Israelites began to whisper that the local
Baalim were angry. The God who guarded them in the
desert had, they thought, forsaken them in the fields.

Thus at one time, even outside Jerusalem, and within sight of the great Temple of Solomon, horrible child sacrifices were made to the hideous Moloch, or Molech, when the crowds sang and beat drums to drown the cries of the dying children.

The *Book of Kings, Chronicles, Judges, Jeremiah* and *Hosea* are full of this terrible clash between Jehovah and the Baalim:

"Hast thou seen what back-sliding Israel hath done?" the Lord asked Jeremiah. "She is gone up on every high mountain and under every green tree and there hath played the harlot."

These "high places of Baal," so often mentioned in the Bible, were pagan shrines on the mountain tops where, among groves of trees and before blood-stained altars, the Canaanites and the back-sliding Israelites indulged in unspeakable rites whose very memory has fortunately vanished from the world.

In order to understand Jezebel, it is necessary to appreciate the religious conflict between the worship of Jehovah and that of the Baalim. For twenty-seven years Jezebel strove to overthrow the God of Israel and to establish the nature worship of her native country, Phoenicia.

She was the daughter of Ethbaal, King of Phoenicia. A political alliance between Israel and the small, but influential, seafaring kingdom was cemented by her marriage to Ahab, King of Israel.

She had inherited from her father, who had been a high priest of Astarte, a strong religious zeal. She was also the typical Oriental despot who took murder in her stride towards any desired objective.

The incident of Naboth's vineyard illuminates this side of her character. Ahab, her husband, desired the vineyard of Naboth, a piece of land that stood next to the royal palace at Jezreel.

Naboth refused to sell his land, and the king, being an Israelite, understood his desire to retain his patrimony. He therefore ceased to bargain but took to his bed, turned his face to the wall and refused food.

Jezebel, a foreigner, declined to see any reason in Naboth's refusal. She had come from a country where the wishes of royalty were never questioned. She was a woman whose authority was absolute:

"Arise and eat bread, and let thine heart be merry," she cried to her husband. "I will give thee the vineyard of Naboth the Jezreelite."

The criminal records of all countries prove how true this is to nature. Behind many of the world's greatest crimes stands a woman like Jezebel urging a weak man on to commit that which he would never have had the courage to commit by himself. In literature one ranks

Jezebel with Clytemnestra and Lady Macbeth.

Naboth was falsely charged with blasphemy, for which the penalty in Israel was a horrible death by stoning. He was therefore flung from a high place and stoned until the life was beaten out of him.

This crime caused such horror throughout the country that the awful prophecy was pronounced that the time would come when "the dogs shall eat Jezebel by the wall of Jezreel."

Like the foreign wives of Solomon, Jezebel established the idolatry of her own country at her husband's court. But she was not content with this. She wished to convert Israel to Baal worship.

Two great sanctuaries were established, one at Samaria and the other at Jezreel. Four hundred and fifty priests of Baal ministered at Samaria; four hundred were attached to the temple at Jezreel.

Ahab, who was entirely under the thumb of his fanatical wife, permitted the prophets of Jehovah to be driven out, and he allowed the worshippers of Baal to overflow the country. So Jezebel became the first religious persecutor in history.

Her husband died in battle. Her sons succeeded to the throne, but for ten years she remained the real power in Israel. She married her daughter, Athaliah, to the King of Judah. Athaliah had inherited her mother's fanaticism, and she introduced to the southern kingdom the Baal worship which her mother was striving with such terrible success to establish over the northern kingdom.

One man alone defeated her—Elijah, a prophet who rose up at this crisis in history and saved the nation from heathenism. A fiery prophet and a patriot, his ruling passion was love for God and his faith in the destiny of Israel.

The moral indignation of this great man burns its way through the *Book of Kings.* Just as Herod stood appalled by the gaunt figure of John the Baptist, so Jezebel shrank from the tremendous personality of Elijah: the man who prophesied that the dogs should eat her body by the wall of Jezreel.

The death of Jezebel is among the most dramatic incidents in the Bible.

The instrument of vengeance was Jehu, a cavalry officer famous for his chariot driving, who agreed to lead a revolt against the hated queen and her sons.

The description of the watchmen on the tower of Jezreel, who, seeing the furious Jehu approaching, knew him by the speed of his driving, is tremendously graphic; so also is the picture of the queen, now no longer a young woman, who leans from her window to watch the coming of the men destined to bring down her house in ruin.

"She painted her face and tired her head and looked out at a window."

It is the one touch of grandeur in her life, and yet, strangely enough, posterity has misinterpreted this dignified act, so that "a painted Jezebel" has for centuries been a bitter taunt. But Jezebel did not paint her face from any motive of coquetry or vanity. She knew that death was ready to take her. Therefore she determined to die like a queen.

Just as Cleopatra, when on the point of death, robed herself in festal garments, so Jezebel painted her eyes with antimony and placed her jewelled crown upon her head; then, mounting to the palace tower, she watched the thundering advance of Jehu's chariot.

As he slowed down to enter the city gate, Jezebel's voice taunted him from the window of the tower:

"Is it peace, thou Zimri, thou murderer of thy master?" she asked.

She meant: "There is no peace for you, Jehu, as there is no peace for me. You may murder me, but your time will also come."

Jehu, furious at the taunt, saw two eunuchs leaning at the window beside the queen. He shouted up to them: "Who is on my side? Who?"

They thrust their beardless faces towards him.

"Throw her down!" he ordered.

And the two slaves caught Jezebel and cast her from

the window before his chariot, "and some of her blood was sprinkled on the wall, and on the horses; and he trod her under foot."

So died Jezebel, the tyrant, the murderess, the fanatic, the woman whom posterity has never ceased to deride for the things she did not do. Impossible as it is to whiten her character, one must point out that she was not, as every dictionary says, a shameless or abandoned woman. Her crimes were not of that kind.

When Jehu entered the palace over the dead body of Jezebel he ate and drank; then, remembering the dead queen, said:

"Go, see now this cursed woman, and bury her."
"And they went to bury her; but they found no more of her than the skull, and the feet, and the palms of her hands."

The horrible prophecy had been fulfilled.

Esther

So FAR, the women of the Bible have had one feature in common: they have all lived in Palestine. With Esther we travel far from that country. We are surrounded by strange customs and we enter a strange court: for the story of Esther is a romance of the captivity in Persia.

The *Book of Esther* permits us, in a remarkable way, to lift the curtain of history and to see what was happening to the conquered tribes in exile. We observe a curious thing. We see a predecessor of Hitler, for we find ourselves in a country that hates the aliens within its gates and decides to rid itself of them.

But the first sign of the dreadful cruelty that has been so often visited upon Israel is seen in the *Book of Esther* when Haman, the prime minister of King Ahasuerus, says to his master:

"There is a certain people scattered abroad and dispersed among the people in all the provinces of thy kingdom; and their laws are diverse from all people; neither keep they the king's laws, therefore it is not for the king's profit to suffer them. If it please the king, let it be written that they may be destroyed."

The king replied to his Hitler:
"Do with them as it seemeth good to thee."
And at that moment Esther wrote her name for ever on the tragic records of her race.

Esther was an orphan of great charm and beauty, who had been brought up by a wise old man called Mordecai. Entering the royal court she had achieved supreme power through one of those Arabian Night reverses of fortune which have occurred so often in Eastern palaces.

[144]

The king had put away his queen for disobedience, and, wishing to choose a successor, had marshalled all the maidens of the land in order that he might inspect them. His choice fell upon the beautiful Esther.

Now, Esther, as a Jewess, a member of the hated captive people, would, no doubt, have been ineligible for the royal honour; so her clever guardian, Mordecai, made the girl promise that she would not reveal her nationality to the king. And to this she agreed.

And the king loved Esther above all the women, and she obtained grace and favour in his sight more than all the virgins; so that he set the royal crown upon her head, and made her queen instead of Vashti.

The ancient chronicler takes us very vividly into the strange, barbaric splendour of the court of Ahasuerus. We enter in imagination that splendid palace of Darius of which nothing now remains but a few uneasy mounds of earth. It was a palace approached by great flights of steps, guarded by enormous stone bulls with human faces and curled beards. Vast pillars, sixty feet in height, ran the length of its halls.

In this palace sat the greatest autocrat of his time, surrounded by his guards, a man whose most foolish afterthought was a command, and into whose presence it was a crime to come unbidden. Beside him sat the Jewish queen, Esther, guarding her secret.

Nine years after Esther became queen—she would then have been about twenty-four—Haman declared his war on the Jews. During those nine years Esther had managed to save the king's life by warning him of a plot revealed to her by Mordecai.

Mordecai, cut off completely from his ward and unpopular because of his nationality, had never received any recognition for his services. When the order went out, however, that all the Jews were to be massacred on the 14th day of Adar—about the end of February—Mordecai decided to approach Esther and beg her to influence the king in favour of the Jews.

Now, the lesson of Esther's story is this: that when a person has gone up in the world and has achieved a position of power and eminence, it requires strength and beauty of character for that person still to love and remember the simple people from whom he, or she, sprang. Humble girls have often married rich men and have forgotten their origin. They have, in fact, been ashamed of anything that might remind them of it.

One imagines that when Mordecai approached Esther after nine years of separation he must have asked himself the question: "Has she changed? Is she too high and mighty now to remember me and all our suffering people?"

The human drama of the *Book of Esther* is that of a woman who was willing to imperil not only her position but her life, out of loyalty and love for her own people.

There was a law that no one might enter the king's presence under penalty of death unless the king extended to him the golden sceptre as a sign that he might advance to the throne. In other words, it was impossible to see him without an appointment.

It was this dangerous breach of etiquette that Esther undertook: "I will go in unto the king," she said, "which is not according to the law; and if I perish, I perish."

In few words we are told how Esther "put on her royal apparel" and drew aside the curtain at the far end of the great throne-room.

We can imagine how the stolid Nubian guards would lower their spears, and how a whisper would run round the hall. Would the golden sceptre be lowered before her? With high courage, the beautiful queen walked slowly across the enormous marble floor towards the throne.

And it was so, when the king saw Esther the queen standing in the court, that she obtained favour in his sight: and the king held out to Esther the golden sceptre that was in his hand. So Esther drew near, and touched the top of the sceptre. Then the king said unto her, What wilt thou, queen Esther? and what is thy request?

With supreme restraint, Esther did not, as most men would have done at such a moment, explain her mission. Instead, with true feminine skill, she told the king that she had prepared a banquet for him and for his Prime Minister.

Esther's "banquet of wine" lasted for two days. When the king had retired after the first night he was unable to sleep; therefore a scribe was called to read over certain official documents to him.

As it happened, the records were those of the plot against his life revealed by Mordecai; and the king remembered that he had not rewarded the faithful Jew.

When Haman came in the morning, the king uttered one of those devastating riddles so characteristic of the Oriental despot.

"What shall be done unto the man whom the king delighteth to honour?" he asked.

Haman, who thought that the king referred to himself, suggested a triumphal procession. The king readily agreed, and ordered him to arrange such a procession for Mordecai.

On the second night of the banquet Esther skilfully worked on the sympathy and affection of the king who, by this time, was in a good humour.

She revealed her nationality. She told the king that a man had designs on her life and on those of her people.

"Who is he and where is he," cried the king, "that durst presume in his heart to do so?"

Esther pointed to Haman, who instantly fell from

favour. The wretched man begged for his life, but Ahasuerus, in one of his violent rages, ordered him to be
hanged. And at the same time Esther obtained from the
king a reversal of the order for a general massacre of
her people.

Esther is one of the most attractive women in the
Old Testament. She is a mixture of charm and strength,
guile and heroism.

Modern morality does not admire the terrible revenge that Mordecai, when in power, took upon the
Medes and Persians, nor the vengeful attitude adopted
by Esther herself. But that is either true to the spirit of
a time which we cannot appreciate, or else it is the in-
vention of an over-patriotic scribe.

As an historical character, Esther is the supreme heroine who delivers her nation from disaster; as a woman,
she is that rare individual: a human being whose character is secure from the rot of wealth, prosperity, and
power.

The Woman of Samaria

ON ONE occasion, when Jesus was returning to Galilee from Jerusalem, we are told by St. John that He took the unpopular road through Samaria.

It was unpopular because the Jews and the Samaritans hated one another. The feud dated back to the Exile, when certain Israelites who had been left behind in

Samaria inter-married with the Assyrian invaders.

After half a century of exile the tribe of Judah returned from Babylon (to be known in future as Jews), and began to rebuild the ruined Temple of Solomon at Jerusalem.

The Jews contemptuously declined the help of the Samaritans on the ground that these people were cross-bred. The insult was never forgiven. The Samaritans set up a rival temple on Mount Gerizim, and from that moment the Jews had no dealings with the Samaritans.

To this day the descendants of the Samaritans, about fifty in number, live in Samaria and at Passover still sacrifice lambs near the ruins of their ancient temple. By a strange revenge of time they are now regarded as the most pure-bred people in the world.

In the time of Christ, however, the feud between Jew and Samaritan was in full swing. The Samaritans way-laid Jewish pilgrims who crossed their territory and maltreated them, while the Jews regarded the Samaritans as Levitically unclean, and made elaborate plans in order to avoid any contact with them.

The revolutionary character of Christ's doctrine is seen vividly in His attitude to the Samaritans. All His references to them are kindly. The parable of the Good Samaritan has made the term a byword for compassion.

A Hitlerite, who at this moment made friendly refer-

ences to German Jews, could not more violently op-
pose popular feeling than Jesus did when He said kind
things about the Samaritans. And it was to a woman of
that detested race that Jesus first confided the secret of
His Divinity.

Weary from His journey, Jesus came down from the
brown hills of Ephraim into the hot Vale of Shechem.
If, as some think, St. John reckoned time not by the
Jewish, but by the Roman, method, it would be six
o'clock in the evening, a time when every rock gives
out its heat before the shadows lengthen and the cool
winds of night come down from the hills.

At the entrance to the green valley Jesus and His
disciples saw the ancient Well of Jacob. This well is still
there. You can see the grooves worn in the stone by the
ropes of women who long ago let down their pitchers
into the well. A little Greek church stands over it to-
day, but when Jesus came to it on His way to Galilee
the well was in the open air.

The disciples set off to buy food in Sychar, a village now called Askar, leaving behind them, one feels
sure, St. John, whose account of what followed has the
authentic brilliance and detail of one who witnessed
and heard.

Crossing the fields from the direction of Sychar came
a Samaritan woman with a pitcher on her shoulder. She

was a woman who had been passed from man to man.

Centuries ago, in small villages like Sychar, as in small villages and towns to-day, a woman with a past was happier alone or in the company of men than in the society of her own sex. Women find it easier to forgive sin in men than in women.

That was probably why this woman of Samaria tramped to the Well of Jacob to draw water rather than to the well nearer the village where, at that time in the evening, all the girls of Sychar would be gathered, ready, no doubt, to snub her.

As she approached the Well of Jacob, she saw a Stranger sitting there. She knew He was a Jew because of His fringed garments. Therefore, when He spoke to her she was surprised. Still more surprising was the fact that He asked a favour.

"Give me to drink," He said.

The woman looked at Him with surprise and suspicion.

"How is it," she asked, "that thou, being a Jew, askest drink of me, which am a woman of Samaria? for the Jews have no dealings with the Samaritans."

The surprising Stranger then replied in words which a modern translator of the Gospels—Dr. James Moffatt —has rendered.

"If you knew what is the free gift of God, and who is asking you for a drink, you would have asked him instead and he would have given you 'living water.'"

The words surprised the Woman of Samaria; and their full meaning has only recently been realized. Jesus was always pointing to things happening round Him to illustrate His words. For instance, when He mentioned the city set upon a hill He was preaching on the shores of Galilee, and He pointed up to the town of Safed which frowns above the lake on the mountains, one of the highest towns in Palestine. When He compared the Scribes and Pharisees to "whited sepulchres," He was speaking from the Court of the Temple in Jerusalem, with thousands of newly whitewashed graves lying below Him in the Kedron Valley, for it was Passover time, when all graves were whitened.

And so He pointed to Jacob's Well, comparing its still waters to the living water of faith. It was only a few years ago that archaeologists, exploring this well, discovered that it was not really a spring of living water, like others in the neighbourhood, but a cistern of dead water, chiefly rain-water and water that had filtered through the strata.

A woman who had held her own with five men was not easily worsted in conversation. She said jokingly:

"Sir, you have nothing to draw water with, and it is a deep well; where do you get your 'living' water? Are you a greater man than Jacob, our ancestor? He gave us this well, and he drank from it, with his sons and his cattle."

The Stranger answered, again pointing to the well:

"Anyone who drinks this water will be thirsty again, but anyone who drinks the water I shall give him will never thirst any more; the water I shall give him will turn into a spring of water, welling up to eternal life."

The woman, still failing to understand, replied mockingly:

"Sir, give me this water, that I thirst not, nor come hither to draw."

The Stranger cut short the argument with a command that went straight to her heart.

"Go, call thy husband," He said, "and come hither."

Much paper has been covered by learned men in an attempt to decide why Jesus should have asked for the woman's husband. It has been considered unworthy to believe that He asked this question, knowing well that the woman had no husband, in order to shame and awaken her to sin.

But surely it is easier to think that Jesus saw in this

ordinary, sinful creature, as He saw in so many other sinners, something beautiful and something worth while; and that, in order to bring her from a proud argumentative attitude of mind into the humility of confession, He asked the one question that opened her heart?

"I have no husband," said the Woman of Samaria. Having said this, she became a different woman. There was no note of hardness or raillery in her again.

"Thou has well said," remarked Jesus gently. "For thou hast had five husbands; and he whom thou now hast is not thy husband."

"Sir, I perceive that thou art a prophet," whispered the woman.

In the marvellous way in which He always spoke to the humble and the simple of heart, Jesus told the Woman of Samaria the divine secret of his Messiahship.

This ordinary, sinful woman stands out among Bible women as the first person to hear from the lips of Christ the story of His mission on earth.

"The woman then left her water-pot, and went her way into the city, and saith to the men, Come, see a man, which told me all things that ever I did: is not this the Christ?"

The Samaritans came running from Askar to see the Reader of Minds. And Jesus said to His disciples:

"Say not ye, There are yet four months, and then cometh harvest? behold, I say unto you, Lift up your eyes, and look on the fields; for they are white already to harvest."

This verse has generally been taken to refer to the time of the year. But surely Jesus, again directing attention to the things around Him, was pointing to the crowd in their white garments who, led by the Woman of Samaria, were running to see Him.

Martha and Mary

I HAVE TAKEN the following brief account of two of the most famous of all New Testament women from my book, *In the Steps of the Master*. I describe going down from Jerusalem towards the Dead Sea and arriving on the way at the little village of Bethany.

The Arab, who turned out to be the sheikh of Bethany, led me in silence over a narrow path between the haphazard walls of piled boulders. We came to a little door in a wall which he unlocked, then, groping in his robes, he found the end of a candle which he lighted and gave to me, and, pointing down into the darkness, said in English, "The Tomb of Lazarus."

This used to be a Christian church and one of the most hallowed and ancient of the holy places in Palestine, but at some later period the Moslems seized it and turned it into a mosque, which still stands above the tomb. Entrance to the tomb was forbidden to Christians for centuries and the old entrance was blocked up. In the seventeenth century the Father Custos of the Holy Land, Angelo of Messina, managed, by paying a fat bribe, to open this new door.

We descended about twenty steps into a dark and dusty cave. The flame of the candle lit up a little vestibule and the ruins of a Christian altar. Two steps lower than this vestibule was a small tomb chamber which is the traditional spot from which Christ recalled Lazarus to life. It is an interesting thing that the modern Arabic name for Bethany is el Azareyh, a form of Lazarus or Eleazar. I stumbled up into the sunlight and, getting rid of the sheikh, went up the hill and sat under one of the many olive trees that grow round it.

There is no doubt at all that this is Bethany, although the House of Mary and Martha and the House of Simon the Leper, which the sheikh is only too happy to show you for a coin, cannot possibly be authentic. This huddle of old stones, however, now inhabited by a few Moslem families, stands on the spot which Jesus knew as Bethany—"the Home of Dates." All one can say is that somewhere on the hill was the house in which Martha, Mary, and their brother, Lazarus, lived.

I think that the character study of Martha and Mary is, as a piece of writing, one of the marvels of literature. There is not one word we could do without, yet the picture is complete, and framed, as it were, by a kitchen door. St. Luke tells it in ninety-eight words:

". . . a certain woman named Martha received him into her house. And she had a sister called Mary, which also sat at Jesus' feet, and heard his word. But Martha was cumbered about much serving, and came to him, and said, Lord, dost thou not care that my sister hath left me to serve alone? bid her therefore that she help me. And Jesus answered and said unto her, Martha, Martha, thou art careful and troubled about many things· but one thing is needful: and Mary hath chosen that good part, which shall not be taken away from her."

Sitting on the little hill above Bethany I could visualize the scene: the house with the smell of cooking around it, for the Feast of Tabernacles, at which this incident occurred, was a busy time for Jewish women, and the little arbour of green leaves—the Tabernacle of the feast—beneath which Jesus would be sitting in the courtyard with Mary at His feet.

They would both be able to see and hear Martha busy with her pots and pans, and she would see Jesus and Mary, so cool and idle while she was so busy. How well her irritation is conveyed by the fact that she includes Jesus in her rebuke! . . . "Lord, dost thou not care that my sister hath left me to serve alone?" She might have said, "Lord, see how my sister doth leave me to serve alone." But she is too angry.

If they had been invisible from her kitchen she might not have been so angry. She would not have seen her sister so cool and tidy, so calm and so intelligent. But Jesus and Mary were sitting in the courtyard in a leafy summer-house of fresh boughs, the peace that surrounded them and the shade in which they sat throwing into relief her own labours, quickening her self-pity and her sense of injustice.

As Martha stands before Jesus we know her so well. She is immortal and international. In every language under the sun, and in every age, Martha has broken into a discussion with an indignant: "You sit there doing nothing while I am working my fingers to the bone!"

And the reply she receives from the arbour is enough to bring tears to her eyes. "Martha, Martha," says Jesus, mentioning her name twice, and thus putting great af-

fection into what followed, "thou art careful and troubled about many things: but one thing is needful: and
Mary hath chosen that good part, which shall not be
taken away from her."

What a play of ideals is here. We might interpret
these words as: "Martha, Martha, you are busy with
many courses when one dish would be quite sufficient.
Mary has chosen the best dish, which shall not be taken
away from her."

And how marvellously St. John takes up the brush
and fills in little details of this character study! When
Jesus came up from Jericho to raise Lazarus, it was the
energetic and practical Martha, who, "as soon as she
heard that Jesus was coming, went and met Him: but
Mary sat still in the house." This is a superbly life-like
touch.

The mystical Mary is still mourning her brother,
but the practical Martha has dried her tears.

"Lord," began Martha, in her usual blunt way, "if
thou hadst been here, my brother had not died." Then,
revealing real depths of her soul, she says, "But I know,
that even now, whatsoever Thou wilt ask of God, God
will give it Thee." And it was to this depth of faith in
Martha that Jesus spoke those words that have brought
comfort and hope wherever a man, or a woman, has stood
above an open grave:

"I am the resurrection, and the life," He said to

Martha. "He that believeth in Me, though he were dead, yet shall he live."

Once again there is a flash of portraiture. Jesus calls for Mary. Martha goes "secretly" to her sister, saying, "The Master is come, and calleth for thee." Unlike Martha, who went dry eyed, Mary runs weeping to fall down in passionate sorrow at the Master's feet.

Not only are the opposite temperaments of these two women drawn with a touch that surely the most obdurate critic must recognize as a painting from life, but also the fact is indicated in the most subtle way that Jesus, while He recognizes that their temperaments are poles apart, loves and understands both of them and thinks no less of one than of the other.

The last scene in which the women of Bethany play a part is just before the Crucifixion. This time it is Mary whose sensitiveness sees what even the disciples do not see, and once again St. John draws a scene that, one feels, he must have witnessed, no matter what some learned commentators may say.

"There they made Him a supper; and Martha served. . . . Then took Mary a pound of ointment of spikenard, very costly, and anointed the feet of Jesus, and wiped His feet with her hair; and the house was filled with the odour of the ointment."

How truly drawn again are the characters of the women: Martha busily supervising the meal, Mary forgetful of the material things, anxious only to pay a tribute to the spiritual.

And how clearly we see the mean, hard face of Judas: "Why was not this ointment sold for three hundred pence, and given to the poor?" he asked.

Dr. Edersheim has estimated that a Roman pound of spikenard such as that used by Mary would have cost nine pounds in modern money. It roused the cupidity of Judas, who made his protest, we learn in a biting aside, "not that he cared for the poor; but because he was a thief, and had the bag, and bare what was put therein."

Then Jesus, rounding off the perfect story of Martha and Mary, spoke over her adoring head what has been called the loneliest sentence in literature:

"Let her alone," He said. "Against the day of my burying hath she kept this."

Herodias

HERODIAS, the mother of Salome, glides like an evil spirit through the Gospel story. She it was who commanded her daughter to ask from Antipas the head of John the Baptist.

If we had nothing more than the brief mention of her in the Gospels, it would be impossible to paint a full-length portrait of her. She would remain for ever a vengeful shadow.

But we do know quite a lot about her from ancient history, and everything we know substantiates the terrible portrait which St. Mark outlines with a few stark words.

Before she joined her evil life with that of Herod Antipas—the Herod of the Trial and Crucifixion—she was living in Rome with her husband, Herod Philip, and their daughter, Salome.

Her husband had been exiled and disinherited because his mother had taken part in a plot against his father, Herod the Great.

Unlike so many of his luckless brothers, he had the good fortune to escape from the untidy shambles of his father's court and to retire into a wealthy private life in Rome. That is all we know about him.

The Herods were intermarried in the most fantastic fashion, believing that no other family was good enough for them, and, as they handed on the same family names with monotonous regularity, their family tree is one of the most puzzling in history.

Herodias and her husband were both related to Herod the Great. She was a granddaughter. Herod Philip was a son. Therefore husband and wife were uncle and niece, or rather half-uncle and half-niece; because Herod had ten wives, and these two people were related only on the male side.

While they were in Rome a relative came to stay with them. He was Philip's half-brother, Herod Antipas, the tetrarch of Galilee, who earned from Jesus the title of "that fox."

It is clear that Herodias, who inherited the blood of many passionate ancestors, was a woman of overmastering ambition.

The quiet life of a Roman matron did not appeal to her. Perhaps she had married Philip in the hope that he would succeed to the blood-stained throne of Judaea, and may be her love, if such emotion may be attributed to Herodias, cooled when her husband stood no longer on the steps of the throne.

Into her comfortable life in Rome came her relative Herod Antipas, a weak, dissolute, timid, cunning man, but one who had inherited under his father's will Galilee and Peraea.

If her first thought was one of hate because Antipas stood where she and her husband should have stood, her second thought was: "Why should this man not give me the power and the position that I want?"

The fact that Antipas was already married did not trouble Herodias. Her ruthless ambition overswept such obstacles. All she saw was the fact that, if she deserted her husband and persuaded the susceptible Antipas to divorce his wife and marry her, she could re-enter as the wife of a ruling prince that country from which she was banished.

The result of their intrigue was that Antipas agreed to divorce his wife, the daughter of the King of Petra, and the next thing we know is that Herodias and her daughter Salome have left Rome and are living in the palace of Antipas.

The wife of Antipas fled back to her father's people, who instantly declared war on the tetrarch. Thus Herod Antipas plunged his Kingdom into strife on behalf of the woman who became his evil genius.

More serious, however, than a tribal war, was the muttering of the Jewish people, who detested and feared such incestuous marriages. Such unions were against the Law of Moses. A preacher garbed in raiment of camel's hair, with a leather girdle about his loins, strode to the foot of the throne and thundered:

"It is not lawful for thee to have thy brother's wife!"

It was the Voice of the People. Antipas was frightened. Herodias was not. She began to hate the Baptist, as she hated anything in her path. John was flung into prison, and Herodias waited her chance.

It came one night when Herod and his army were encamped on the heights of Machaerus, a cone-shaped hill thousands of feet above the Dead Sea. It was the frontier fortress that guarded the approach to Petra. Below the castle, in whose dungeons St. John was lying, lay a large town built round a palace that Herod the Great created with infinite labour among the mountains of Moab.

It was Herod's birthday—or perhaps the anniversary of his accession—a time when it was customary for him to grant favours. He had feasted with his State officials and his army officers.

It was evidently a men's banquet. Even Herodias was not present. But she was not far away when, through the hangings at the end of the banquet hall, Salome moved forward to the sound of drums and flutes.

The dance in the East has never been a respectable occasion. Salome was a princess of the royal house. It was not the beauty of Salome that captivated Herod: it was her astonishing act of abasement that appealed to his perverted mind.

"And she went forth and said unto her mother, What shall I ask?"

Herodias replied:

"The head of John the Baptist."

In a few moments the executioner had done his work. In hideous mockery the head of the saint was placed upon a plate, as if it had been a feature of the meal, and given to Salome. A legend says that when Herodias saw it she bent forward and thrust a bodkin through the tongue that had dared to challenge her.

The Gospels do not tell us whether Herodias sat

beside Herod Antipas when Jesus was robed in mockery and sent back to Pilate; in fact, the Gospels mention her no more.

But we are able to follow her career in ancient history, and there we see how her ambition and her lust for power drove her husband into ruin. And it came about in a strange manner.

The bad boy of the Herodian House was a gay young bankrupt called Agrippa, who, when he was not in search of moneylenders, was escaping from them. He was the brother of Herodias. In Rome, where more than once he saw the inside of a prison, he became the bosom friend of the mad young prince, Caligula. They were in the habit of roystering round Rome together disguised in long cloaks.

When Caligula was made emperor, Agrippa was suddenly released from prison, where he had been serving a short sentence, was loaded with honours and riches and made Tetrarch of Batanaea, with the title of king.

This kingdom lay next to Galilee. Therefore, Herodias, who had always wished to be a queen, was forced to accept as her neighbour, and bend the knee to, the ne'er-do-well brother and her sister-in-law, Berenice.

This was too much for Herodias. It was more than her proud, violent nature could stand. She so worked on the feelings of the miserable Antipas that he agreed to go with her to Rome to put the injustice of the case before the Emperor. It was the most foolish thing she could have done.

Her brother, Agrippa, heard of the journey and sent swift messengers ahead to Rome with the secret information that Antipas had smuggled sufficient arms into Galilee to fit out an army of seventy thousand. When Antipas and Herodias came into the presence of Caesar they were questioned about the arms. Caligula did not like their answers.

In one of his sudden mad rages, he banished both Antipas and Herodias and—gave their tetrarchy to Agrippa! It was then that Herodias proved that some spark of courage and splendour may exist in the worst of characters.

The Emperor offered her freedom and all her possessions because she was the sister of his friend, but with a flash of Maccabean pride the woman scornfully refused the favour. She preferred to go into exile, poor and disgraced, with the man whose life she had ruined.

It is said that the place of exile was Lyons, in Gaul. So this man and woman who slew St. John the Baptist, and had it in their power to save the life of Christ, depart together into the mists of history. Legend says that they died in Spain.

Bethlehem

He came al so still
  To his mother's bour,
As dew in April
  That falleth on the flour.

He came al so still
  There his mother lay,

As dew in April
      That falleth on the spray.

Mother and maiden
      Was never none but she;
Well may such a lady
      Goddes mother be.

A Fifteenth-Century Carol.

IN THE starlight of a night long ago, when Herod the Great was King of Judaea, the roads of Palestine were crowded with reluctant travellers. The great trunk road, on which the silks and the candied fruits of Damascus met the pickled fish of Galilee and the gold of Arabia, was that night alive with families travelling on camel-back, on asses, and on foot.

Villages and towns were awake all through the land. A cluster of lights marked Nazareth on its hill. The stark little towns of Judaea gleamed darkly among the clefts of the mountains; and on the flat land of the Sharon Plain lanterns shone against the background of the sea like the camp fires of a host.

Dusty and travel weary, the wayfarers came to towns and villages and knocked upon doors. Alas, some had nowhere to sleep that night. Guest chambers were full, and travellers, finding no room in the khans or in the houses of their friends and relatives were shown into lofts and garrets and stables.

There were some who grumbled as they slaked their thirst and broke their fast:

"God knoweth our numbers, Why should we be counted on the fingers of men?"

God knoweth our numbers . . . It was the old cry of Israel, the hatred of the counting of heads, the sin that drove David to build an altar unto the Lord on the threshing-floor of Ornan the Jebusite. But these were different times.

Augustus, the Master of the World, had sent forth a decree that men should be counted, and Herod the King had commanded that all Jews, men and women, should return into their tribal territory and be enrolled as households, as the Egyptians were enrolled every fourteen years for the ease and convenience of the tax collector.

Men spat upon the floor and cursed the disjointed world. Some day, they said, a king would rise in Israel, the Messiah, a man sprung from the loins of David, one born with a sword in his hand, a man of war, and he would free his country and drive the oppressor into the sea.

Among those who travelled from Nazareth at the time of the census was Joseph the Carpenter, and Mary,

[177]

his wife. They were on their way to Bethlehem, David's Town, because Joseph was of the house and family of David.

Among the women who travelled the roads that night there must have been many like Mary of Nazareth over whom hovered the mystery of birth. Greater even than any mystery of motherhood was the mystery of her destiny and the sacred mystery of the splendour that was so soon to fall upon her.

As Mary rode that night to Bethlehem, one is reminded of the opening words of *Genesis*. Once again in the history of the world the Spirit is brooding on the face of the waters, and as its wings go past in the darkness they promise new hope for the human soul.

"From henceforth," Mary had cried in the Magnificat, "all generations shall call me blessed." She had not singled out one nation from the others. Her song was the first expression of the unity of Mankind, the first cry for the abolition of injustice and inequality and greed, the first looking forward to a better world.

So the immortal travellers came out of Samaria, and as they climbed up into the foothills of Judaea they approached the long steep road that leads to Jerusalem, and saw a city, cruel and dark within its wall, crouched in the night like those beasts which the Egyptians carved on their temples.

If they came down by the north road, where the white

towers of Hippicus and Phasaël gleamed on their right, they would have passed a little hill outside the city gate. The name of this hill was Golgotha.

The road to Bethlehem runs like a white ribbon for five miles to the south of Jerusalem.

The little town which the travellers now approached, climbed the hill among olives and vines. Beneath the fateful stars of that night Joseph and Mary went from house to house seeking a lodging, for from far and near, all the tribe of David was crowded together in that place.

The old houses in Bethlehem are built above caves in the rock. Above these caverns, where the cattle are stabled at night, are the rooms where the humble families live. In such a dwelling Mary of Nazareth found a lodging.

There was no place for her in the room above; but below in the friendly darkness of the rock, and among the quiet, friendly beasts of the field, the mother of Jesus made her bed that night.

Just outside Bethlehem was a place called Migdal Eder, "the watch-tower of the flocks," where the sacrificial lambs were gathered before they were driven towards Jerusalem, to the altar on which their blood was spilt.

"And there were in the same country shepherds abiding in the field, keeping watch over their flock by night. And, lo, the Angel of the Lord came upon them, and the glory of the Lord shone round about them: and they were sore afraid. And the angel said unto them, Fear not: for, behold I bring

[179]

you good tidings of great joy, which shall be to all people. For unto you is born this day in the city of David a Saviour, which is Christ the Lord.

And this shall be a sign unto you; Ye shall find the babe wrapped in swaddling clothes, lying in a manger. And suddenly there was with the angel a multitude of the heavenly host praising God, and saying, Glory to God in the highest and on earth peace, good will toward men.

The shepherds said, one to the other:

"Let us now go even unto Bethlehem, and see this thing which is come to pass, which the Lord hath made known to us."

There is an ancient story that at this moment mariners off the coasts of Greece heard a voice crying in the darkness: "Great Pan is dead!"

The story of the first Christmas is the most lovely story in the world. It is one on which the world has lavished the treasure of its love and its imagination: the shepherds on their knees, the Wise Men with their gifts, the quiet beasts in the dusk of the cave where the Mother sat with her Child.

Those who believe in Christ and those who deny Him agree in one thing: that on this first Christmas night long ago in Bethlehem, the first vision of Perfection shone out over the world. The world is still imperfect, but the Vision remains: the vision of a world ruled by love and justice, where man loves God with all his heart and soul and his neighbour as himself.

More precious even than the inspired canvases of Botticelli and Correggio are the little pictures of a frosty night in Bethlehem which each one of us holds in his heart.

The sound of the heavenly host above the Watch Tower of the Flock has been taken up by human voices ever since. It comes to us from the past, and we sing it in the darkness of the present:

Come, all ye faithful, joyful and triumphant,
Come ye, O come ye, to Bethlehem.

Pilate's Wife

A WOMAN OF the Bible whose brief appearance stimulates the imagination is the wife of Pontius Pilate. All we know about her is a passage of thirty-eight words in the Gospel of St. Matthew; but these thirty-eight words are significant.

During the trial of Jesus, when the Governor was sit-

ting in judgment in the Praetorium, a messenger hurried
up to him with a warning from his wife. The message
was brief and urgent. It was the kind of message that
many a wife has sent to her husband in a moment of
crisis.

She had had a dream; and she begged Pilate not to condemn the Prisoner. The exact words of St. Matthew are
worth close study.

> When he was set down on the judgment seat, his wife sent
> unto him, saying, Have thou nothing to do with this just
> man: for I have suffered many things this day in a dream
> because of him.

At first sight, perhaps, this passage would seem to have
no hidden meaning; but when we take it word by word we
learn a number of things. Firstly, it suggests that the judgment hall in which Christ was condemned lay some distance from Pilate's residence, otherwise surely the wife
would herself have presented her urgent petition?

Secondly, the trial must have taken place very early,
and Pilate must have left Government House before
his wife was awake.

Thirdly, Pilate and his wife must have discussed Jesus
together, probably on the night before—the night of the
arrest in the Garden of Gethsemane—because the ur-
gency of her message shows a keen appreciation of the
danger in which He stood.

[184]

The woman whose brief mention in the Gospels throws such interesting light on the Trial and Crucifixion is, alas, one of the most shadowy figures in the Gospels.

Tradition claims that her name was Claudia Procula. She is said to have been a Roman aristocrat and a grand-daughter of the Emperor Augustus. If this were so, it explains why Pilate was able to break the rule that forbade provincial governors to take their wives with them to their provinces.

As wife of the Roman Governor of Judaea, Claudia would have lived in the surroundings of a queen. Rome swooped down and annexed Judaea shortly after the death of that great palace-builder, Herod the Great, and some of the most luxurious buildings in the world were at the disposal of Pilate's wife.

There was the great palace of Caesarea, another in Samaria, and, most splendid of all, the enormous white palace above Jerusalem on which Herod squandered untold wealth.

This building shone with halls of silver and gold and precious marbles. One of its state apartments held couches for three hundred guests. Its gardens were always loud with the sound of running water and the cooing of doves.

In Roman times this palace was closed except on occasions such as the Passover Festival when it was the duty of Pilate to leave his official headquarters at Caesarea, on the sea-coast, and journey up to the capital for ten days with extra troops; for the Jews saved their political demonstrations for Passover Week.

Therefore, once a year we can imagine Pilate and his wife inhabiting a bleak wing of this colossal palace, a palace haunted by the blood-stained ghosts of Herod's court. The great halls in which Herod revelled and plotted were empty and full of shadow.

It must have been a dreary ten days for Pilate and his wife. Pilate disliked and despised the Jews. He hated their fanaticism, their intolerance, and their religious taboos. More than once he had lost his temper and ordered his troops to slaughter them. But he had the respect of an administrator for a Foreign Office which was never reluctant to sacrifice an official to a policy, and for the underground influence of the Jews, and their habit of sending smooth-tongued embassies behind his back to Rome.

We can imagine that, as Pilate and his wife were carried in litters on these occasions into the fiery highlands of Judaea, the Governor would turn to her and say: "I wonder what new trouble will break this year?"

Life must have been lonely for those two Romans in the great empty palace in Jerusalem. Although Herod Antipas and Herodias came up to Jerusalem for the Passover, and stayed probably at the old Ashmonaean Palace, their social contact with Pilate was purely formal. Their relationship was probably not unlike that which might exist between a British Governor and a not too loyal or friendly Rajah.

We can infer from the Gospels that since Pilate had quelled a Galilean riot with the sword, the Governor of Judaea and the native ruler of Galilee had certainly not even pretended to be friends.

Then the Roman population of Jerusalem could not have been large, and it was purely mercantile. It included no one of Pilate's rank. Unless the Governor and his wife invited friends from Rome, or distinguished tourists who might be passing homeward from Egypt through Judaea, to witness the annual sacrifice in the Jewish Temple, their visit must have been purely of an official nature.

The only other Roman of rank in Jerusalem was the *chiliarch,* or commanding officer, of the cohort of the Twelfth Legion, the troops which at that date garrisoned Jerusalem.

This man, who was Pilate's second-in-command, would have met his superior officer with a guard of honour whenever he visited the capital, and his first act would have been to tell Pilate all that was going on: the state of popular feeling, the political situation, the inner politics of the Sanhedrin, and any other matters of special interest that had a bearing on the great annual pilgrimage to Jerusalem, which in those days was to the Jew what the modern pilgrimage of Mecca is to the Moslem.

It is impossible to believe that this officer did not tell

Pilate, the instant he set foot in Jerusalem, of the Sanhedrin's plot to arrest and condemn Jesus Christ.

The Roman secret police must have been aware of this plot. It must have been the common talk of the bazaars. As soon as Jesus drove out the money changers and the hucksters from the Temple court, it must have been common knowledge that Annas, the High Priest, whose family owned this prosperous market, would take legal revenge.

And there is one word in the Gospel of St. John which supports this supposition.

Describing the arrest of Jesus in the Garden of Gethsemane, St. John (in the Greek text) uses the word *chiliarch* to describe the officer in command of the party sent to arrest Jesus.

Now we cannot imagine that the officer commanding a garrison would go in person to effect an arrest except in very extraordinary circumstances. Are we right in supposing that Annas and Caiaphas and the leaders of the Sanhedrin, used their influence with the Roman authorities and, by stressing the political consequences of the case, enlisted the services of the commander?

If so, this implies a carefully prepared plot; and this theory is clearly strengthened by the circumstances of the Trial before Pilate. We have seen that this took place early in the morning. It took place also on a day when the courts were usually shut. It was the time of preparation for the Passover and that was why the Jews who charged Jesus would not cross the threshold of the Gentile Praetorium; for they would suffer ceremonial defilement and be unable to cleanse themselves before the beginning of the feast. We read how Pilate kept going in and coming out to them.

That Pilate rose early before his wife was awake, that he held a court on the eve of a religious festival when the courts were usually closed, argues one important fact: that the High Priest came to him on the night before the trial, knowing perfectly well that the Sanhedrin would condemn Jesus, and said to Pilate:

"Will you be prepared to hold a court early to-morrow to condemn a most dangerous agitator who has been giving us a lot of trouble?"

And the Roman Governor, who alone could pronounce the death sentence since Judaea had become a Roman province, must have agreed.

Could it be possible that Claudia did not learn of all this? What wife could have remained ignorant of it? Pilate's dislike and contempt for the Sanhedrin came out very clearly in the Trial of Jesus, when, time after time, he saw through their cunning plot and was only, at the end, blackmailed by the threat of a complaint to Caesar into weakly condemning Christ to the cross.

[189]

A man of Pilate's temper could not keep his irritation from his wife: he would unburden himself in no uncertain way.

Of all the talks in history, surely that between Pilate and Claudia on the night before the Crucifixion is the most interesting. It was the night of the Last Supper. The night of the Agony in the Garden of Gethsemane.

The hobnailed sandals of the Roman troops had clattered down the rocks into the Valley of the Kedron, and the band, with lanterns on the end of poles and led by Judas, had found their Victim.

In the gaunt, bare palace on the hill, the Roman Governor and his wife were talking in the ghostly silence, sitting perhaps at the end of a vast hall, warming their hands above a brazier.

Did Claudia already know of Jesus? Was she, as some had thought, already a Christian? Had she heard of the miracles in Galilee? Perhaps one of her Jewish maids was a follower, or the relative of a follower, of Jesus?

It is fruitless to wonder, for we shall never know. All we can say is that on the night before the Crucifixion a Roman woman pleaded for the life of Jesus, and that His peril was so much on her mind that she dreamed of Him.

In the morning her first action was to tell her husband of this dream. She awakened. It was late! Perhaps, because of the excitement of the night before, the going and coming of messengers, the news of the arrest, the sudden demand of the High Priest for an urgent interview with Pilate, she had not gone to bed until the small hours.

Wild with anxiety, Claudia sees that Pilate's room is empty. He has already gone to the court. Perhaps at that moment the dreadful thing has happened. She calls a messenger and writes:

Have thou nothing to do with this just man: for I have suffered many things this day in a dream because of him.

The messenger runs off into the streets and down to the Castle of Antonia. Claudia waits . . .

Was she the first European woman who believed in Christ? The Greeks and the Abyssinians have made a saint of her. But impenetrable darkness surrounds her life. She disappears from history.

Legend, however, has been as busy with her name as with that of her husband. Pilate is said to have committed suicide, while Claudia is said to have become a Christian, and has even been identified, perhaps a little recklessly, with the Claudia mentioned by St. Paul in his second letter to Timothy.

Mary Magdalene

ON THE west bank of the Sea of Galilee, not far from the ruins of Capernaum, a few squalid mud hovels stand among palm-trees. Arab women crouch against the mud walls, or draw lake water in empty petrol-tins.

The visitor is instantly surrounded by hordes of half-naked, and generally ophthalmic, children, who hold out

their hands, crying the only English word they know—
"Penny." This miserable little village is called Mejdel.
It is the ancient Magdala. Somewhere, perhaps, under the
unshapely mounds of earth and the piles of black basalt,
lie the ruins of the once prosperous lakeside town which
in ancient days sent its tribute in wagons to the Temple
at Jerusalem.

This was the town of Mary of Magdalene, or Mary of
Magdala, the woman from whom Jesus drove out seven
devils.

Mary Magdalene, one of the most faithful and beautiful characters in the Bible, has been terribly misrepre-
sented by legend. I have just noted that the Concise Ox-
ford Dictionary gives the meaning of "Magdalen" as
"reformed prostitute." Artists, preachers, and others have
pictured her for centuries as the typical penitent weeping for her sins.

There is absolutely nothing in the New Testament to
justify the popular impression of Mary Magdalene,
which, by the way, did not take root until the time of
St. Ambrose, in the fourth century. The early Christian
Church did not regard her as a reformed prostitute. How,
then, did this impression gain credence?

It began with a curious double misunderstanding.
First, "the woman that was a sinner" who anointed the
feet of Jesus in the Galilean Pharisee's house, has, without
the slightest justification, been identified with Mary of

Magdala. Secondly, it has been assumed that "the seven devils" is another expression for the "many sins" in St. Luke's pathetic incident of the anointing.

It would seem clear from other instances recorded in the Gospels and in Hebrew literature that demoniacal possession had nothing to do with morals, but had everything to do with disease and nervous disorder.

In certain instances demoniacal possession was clearly epilepsy. For instance, we learn from St. Mark that when Christ asked a father how long his son had been possessed by a demon, the man answered:

"Of a child. And ofttimes it hath cast him into the fire and into the waters, to destroy him."

But legend, with cruel insistence, has befouled the memory of Mary Magdalene, interpreting the seven demons in moral, and not pathological, terms. The great mediaeval schools of painting immortalized the injustice, and to-day the name Magdalen is a synonym for a woman of the streets.

Geikie expresses the attitude of many scholars when he says: "Never perhaps has a figment so utterly baseless obtained so wide an acceptance."

When Mary Magdalene was cured by Jesus, she turned with joy and thankfulness to join the band of female followers, which included Joanna, the wife of Chuza, Herod's steward, Susanna, Salome, the wife of Zebedee, and Mary, the mother of Jesus.

Without these devoted women, as great and splendid in their own sphere as were St. Peter, St. James, St. John, and St. Andrew, the story of Christ's mission on earth would be incomplete. They followed Jesus along the roads of Palestine, "ministering" to Him and listening to His teaching, conscious maybe of the revolutionary character of that teaching as it affected them and all women who were to come after them.

Mary of Magdala clearly occupied a position of great prominence among the women disciples. It has been suggested that she possessed more worldly goods than most of Christ's followers, and that she was among the women who "ministered unto them of their substance." That, of course, we cannot prove.

We know, however, that among those who went up from Jericho to Jerusalem in the April of the Crucifixion was Mary of Magdala. When the storm broke over the heads of the Apostles they fled, but she and the women followers did not desert Jesus in the hour of His trial and death.

In the Synoptic Gospels her name comes first among the list of women who witnessed the Crucifixion, and from this we are perhaps at liberty to imagine that in that dark hour Mary Magdalene assumed the leadership of the heartbroken band.

St. John's description of her visit to the sepulchre early on the morning of the third day is one of the most beautiful and vivid narratives in literature.

Mary, seeing the empty tomb, believed that friends or foes had stolen away the body of Christ. She saw that the big circular stone that closed the ancient Jewish sepulchres had been rolled back along its groove, leaving the entrance clear. She sped back to tell St. Peter and St. John that some one had stolen the dead Christ.

She ran back to the tomb with them. St. John, who was younger than St. Peter, ran faster and reached the tomb first. He stooped down and looked into the rock-hewn cave; but he did not enter. When St. Peter arrived, he at once entered and St. John followed. They saw the linen graveclothes lying in the sepulchre.

When the two Apostles had departed, Mary Magdalene stayed near the tomb, unable to tear herself away, her heart broken by the thought that the splendid hopes built upon Christ's Ministry should have ended in the shame of crucifixion and the horror of a rifled grave.

As she turned away, she saw through her tears a Figure standing, which she took to be that of the gardener; for the tomb was in a rock garden:

"Woman, why weepest thou? Whom seekest thou?" asked a Voice; and Mary Magdalene, still thinking that she was speaking to the gardener, asked.

"Sir, if thou have borne him hence, tell me where thou hast laid him, and I will take him away."

The Voice said to her: "Mary."

Instantly the cry broke from her, for she had recognized the voice of Jesus:

"Master!"

But, as she prepared to fling herself at His feet, Jesus stayed her with the words.

"Touch me not; for I am not yet ascended to my Father: but go to my brethren, and say unto them, I ascend unto my Father, and your Father; and to my God and your God."

And in the brightness of the sunrise Mary Magdalene ran back through the gates of Jerusalem to tell the disciples that she had spoken to the Christ.

The Rev. Henry Latham, in his beautiful book, *The Risen Master,* has written:

Mary had stayed at the foot of the Cross when the Apostles shrunk away—two only following afar off. What she receives is after the kind of the rewards that our Lord confers—it is no crown of glory, no guerdon that men or women would dream of—she is given a closer knowledge of things divine. When the eyes of others are holden, she discerns the Lord. To Mary Magdalene—and in some degree to women-kind in her person, was given an honour that could not be taken away. To her, first of all living beings, the Risen Lord appeared.

Index

INDEX

INDEX

INDEX